Highlights®
Book
of
Science
Questions
That
Children
Ask

Answered by **Highlights** for Children Science Editor Jack Myers

BARNES
&NOBLE
BOOKS
NEW YORK

ISBN 1-56619-817-8
This edition published by Barnes & Noble Inc. by arrangement
with Boyds Mills Press

1995 Barnes & Noble Books
The text of this book is set in 11-point Century Schoolbook.
The illustrations are done in ink, colored pencils, and watercolors.
10 9 8

Illustrations by Ernest Albanese, Bill Colrus, Mimi Powers, Tom Powers,
Tanya Rebelo, and John Rice.

The text and illustrations in this book originally appeared in *What Makes
Popcorn Pop?, Can Birds Get Lost?, How Do We Dream?,* and *Do Cats Really
Have Nine Lives?* by Jack Myers, copyright © 1991, 1991, 1992, and 1993 by
Boyds Mills Press.

Welcome Aboard!

You have joined our club. We are the curious, wondering about all the interesting things that happen in our world. When we don't know, we ask. Here in the records of our club you will find answers to some of the questions you have wondered about.

For the past thirty years readers of *Highlights for Children* have been asking me questions. And as Science Editor of *Highlights*, I have been helping them find answers. I did not make up these questions so that the answers could teach science. They are questions asked by real people like you. From those questions, and my letters in reply, a few were chosen for publication in "Science Letters," which is a regular column in the magazine. And of those published questions and answers, a fraction have been collected to create this book. The questions have not been changed, except to correct some spelling. So you will find questions you may have asked yourself, in language you might have used.

Finding answers to these questions wasn't all peaches and cream. Of course, lots of answers can be found in books. I have a few shelves of those, and I live near a great library. But I discovered very early that not all the questions you can think of have their answers neatly cataloged in books. Fortunately, I have spent most of my life at a university. In time, my friends there got used to me coming to them for help. I also found that there are many things, especially about nature, that are known only by people such as ranchers and hunters and fishermen who spend their lives outdoors.

In a few cases, I can remember how I found the answers. On page 191 you will find a question about what would happen if you fell into a hole all the way through the earth. My friend Claude Horton is a geophysicist and just the person to help answer that. In fact, he not only helped, he wrote the answer that is in this book. Two other friends, Clark Hubbs and the late Osmond P. Breland, also wrote some of the answers. Their answers are acknowledged by their initials.

On page 18 you will find a question about green polar bears. Everyone knows that polar bears are supposed to be white. You won't find anything about green ones in any encyclopedia. Fortunately, I had seen a friend's article in a scientific magazine that provided the answer.

There is also a question about deer antlers on page 26. Every year, a male deer loses its antlers, and new ones grow. So why aren't there piles of old antlers lying around? I found out the answer from my grandson, Scott Wendlandt. He is a wildlife biologist who is happiest when he is out watching deer.

To all of the many people who aided us, we are grateful, for they have broadened our understanding.

Not everyone will like the answers. Some readers will say that I left some questions unanswered. That's true. There have been questions I could not answer and questions that I think no one could answer. And many of the answers are not snappy "fast food," but rather ideas to chew on. I can only hope you like to chew on ideas.

Science has always been like that, and it is like that today even in the world's greatest laboratories. It is our ignorance—what we don't know—that drives us to learn more. That's what science is all about.

Jack Myers

Jack Myers, Ph.D.

CONTENTS

ANIMALS

BODY AND MIND

THE WORLD

Questions About Animals

As our pets, sometimes as pests, more often as untamed creatures of beauty, animals are always with us. At first, their ways may seem alien or even silly. But with the patience to watch quietly and the willingness to ask questions, we can start to understand them. Each of us can become an amateur naturalist and begin to see the reasons why animals behave as they do. The young naturalists who posed the questions in this section have watched, wondered, and asked. It is likely they have asked some of the same things you have wondered about. They may surprise you with some questions that have not occurred to you. And we hope they will lead you to look around and ask even more new questions of your own.

Questions About Body and Mind

From the wrinkles that form on our fingertips during a bath to the constant flow of images that we call "thinking," the mysteries about ourselves are among the greatest, or at least the most fun. In this section, you will learn about the reasons for some seemingly odd features of the human body. How do we dream? How do we breathe without thinking about it? How does our skin heal a cut? Why do we throw up? Through the answers to these questions, you will discover that your body houses an amazing series of automatic responses that protect your health. Prepare to explore one of nature's most amazing inventions—you.

Questions About the World

From the beginning of human history, people have tried to understand the world around them. They gazed at the sun, moon, and stars, and they came up with ideas about what those objects might be. They thought about the surprising properties of water in all of its forms: ice, liquid, and gas. They studied the orange-red flame of fire and the "fire" that erupts from some mountains. They wondered how a giant tree grows from a tiny seed. Year after year, they compared their ideas with what they saw, and they became better at asking questions, guessing the answers, and testing their guesses against what's real. In this section, you will see that we understand a great deal about many of the things we wonder about. You will also see that many fascinating questions are still unanswered. We still need curious minds like yours to help us understand the universe.

Questions About Animals

How do birds communicate?

Maria Spredbury
FPO, New York

I think most birds communicate by making sounds. There are a large number of sounds made by different species. Some of these are songs. Many more are simpler sounds, like cheeps and quacks and caws and twitters. Birds cannot talk and express ideas the way you and I do, but they can send some simple messages, like "This is my territory," or "Danger, danger," or "I like you."

Some birds communicate also by displays, as a male turkey does when it ruffs up its feathers. I think such displays are usually used in mating.

Animal communication is a big subject for research, so we are learning more all the time.

I have made a birdhouse, but not a bird touches it. I put bird seed in it and mud and grass, but still not a bird goes into it. Could you help me?

Ellie Mendenhall
Omaha, Nebraska

You could try reading about the kinds of birds that live in Nebraska. Find out what kinds of places they like to live and what kinds of food they like to eat. That may help you to place your birdhouse where a bird will be more likely to use it.

Not all kinds of birds like to use birdhouses. And some kinds are very particular. I think little wrens will use only birdhouses with very small holes for openings.

Also, you will find that where you put a birdhouse is important. Birds usually are careful to nest where cats and snakes and squirrels will not be a problem. Birds build their own nests, and each kind does that in its own way. So, I think it may not be a good idea to put grass and mud in it.

My best suggestion is this. Look around town and see who has birdhouses with birds. Then go ask those people for their advice. It will be better than mine.

Once my mom cracked open an egg, and there were two yolks. Can there be two chickens in one egg?

Devon Greyson
Ann Arbor, Michigan

No. Or at least it's not very likely. One reason is that there probably is not enough stored food in the egg to allow two chicks to develop. And I have never found anyone who has actually seen two chicks hatch from one egg.

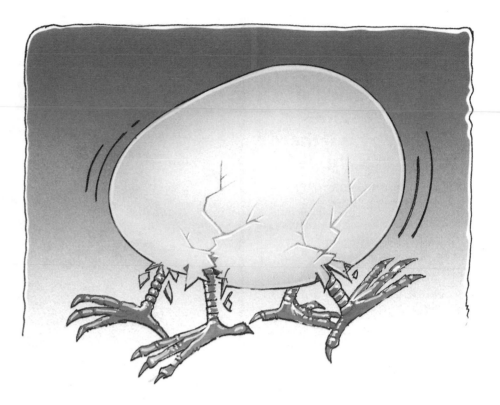

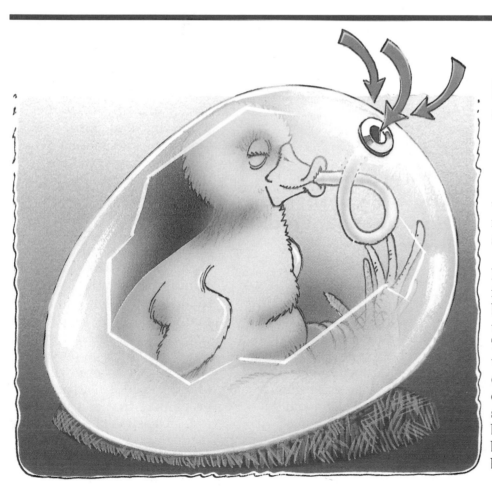

How do baby birds breathe inside their eggs?

Nora Mahlberg
Madison, Wisconsin

I'm glad that you are wondering about some of the many interesting things you see in nature.

A bird's eggshell and the lining inside are very neat inventions. As you know, a baby bird has to start growing up while still inside the egg. The eggshell is good at holding water in so the insides don't dry up. And it allows the gases oxygen and carbon dioxide to seep through. That's how the baby bird does its breathing before it gets big enough to break out of the shell.

13

I live on a ranch. When we have to pull a calf out of the cow, it has a "sack" of phlegm or something. Why is it there? I know colts have it, too.

*Lane Buchanan
Baggs, Wyoming*

I have never actually seen a calf pulled out of a cow at birth. So you know more about this than I do, and I am not sure about what you call a "sack" of phlegm. Maybe what I can tell you will help.

In most mammals the birth process is pretty standard, at least in principle. The baby has developed in the uterus of the mother. It is attached to the wall of the uterus by a special tissue, the placenta. And it is enclosed in two surrounding, fluid-filled sacs.

In squeezing its way out of the uterus, the sac must break. The baby is born still attached by a cord to the placenta. In some way the cord is cut or broken. Then afterwards the placenta, usually called the afterbirth, breaks loose and is also discharged.

All those same things will happen when a baby is born, whether in humans, or cows, or horses. I hope this will help you answer your question.

I would like to know about snakes. How do snakes make babies?

*Franco Tassone
LaSalle, Quebec*

The egg cells of female snakes must be fertilized before they can have babies or lay eggs that will hatch. You may know that some snakes keep the eggs inside and have babies inside their bodies. Others lay their eggs outside. Rattlesnakes, copperheads, moccasins, and garter snakes have babies. Sometimes they have very large families. A snake may have nearly one hundred babies at one time.

Bullsnakes, rat snakes, racers, pythons, and many others lay eggs. One python once laid more than one hundred. How would you like to have a hen that laid this many eggs at one time? Snake eggs are quite different from the eggs of birds and chickens. They have a different shape, and the shell is not easy to break, like that of a chicken's eggs. The shell of a snake's egg is tough and leathery.

O.P.B.

I would like to learn more about the poisonous snakes in the world. The ones I am really interested in are rattlesnakes because my family owns a cabin in the Poconos.

William Sandor
Easton, Pennsylvania

There are several kinds of snakes that are called vipers. Rattlesnakes, copperheads, and the cottonmouth moccasin belong to a group called pit vipers. They get that name because all of them have a small pit or depression between the eye and the nostril on each side. These pits are heat detectors. They help the snake find a smaller animal, such as a mouse, even at night. The pit vipers are poisonous.

There are a dozen or so different kinds of rattlesnakes, most of which live in the southern parts of the United States. I have not had much experience in Pennsylvania. There is a rattler called the massasauga, or swamp rattler, reported from Pennsylvania, and I think also the timber rattler. The copperhead also occurs in Pennsylvania, but none of the other pit vipers.

One is not nearly as likely to find a poisonous snake in Pennsylvania as in many of the southern states. However, when you are in the woods, or walking through the high grass or weeds, you should take some precautions. Don't step over a log until you can see the ground on the other side, and always look before you step. If a rock or log is moved, you should stand well to one side until you can see what is under it. And, of course, you should never stick your hand in a hole in the ground or in a cavity in a tree.

When walking in high grass or weeds, push a stick in front of you before you step. Most poisonous snakes in the United States will crawl away rather than bite, if you give them the chance. Incidentally, as I can tell you from experience, rattlesnakes do not always rattle before they strike.

O.P.B.

I have a question. Do bumblebees make honey?

Jacob Delph
Phoenix, Arizona

Bumblebees are usually yellow and black, larger than honeybees, and look even larger because of a thick covering of hair. Bumblebees do make honey, but only enough to live on during the summer. They are social, which means that many bees live together in a colony.

Usually they live underground, maybe in an old nest left by a field mouse. In a colony there are different kinds, like drones and workers and queens, but they are not as well organized as honeybees.

At least in the northern states, only a few queens live through the winter by finding hiding places in the ground. So, they do not have to make a big store of honey to feed the whole colony during the winter.

When I think about bumblebees, I think of a story often told by my father. He grew up on a farm in southern Pennsylvania. When he was old enough, he was taught to plow. The plow was pulled by a horse or team of horses. The driver walked behind the plow and held onto its two handles to keep it pointed right as it turned over the soil. My father used a big and strong but very slow horse called Kate. The very worst thing that could happen was that the plow would go through a bumblebee nest. Then Kate would stop and stamp her feet. And my father was stuck with a lot of very mad bumblebees. You can see why my father never forgot that experience, even when he became the first editor of HIGHLIGHTS many years later.

How can you tell a butterfly from a moth?

Andy Strain
Brownsburg, Indiana

Moths and butterflies are much alike, and they are classified into the same group or order. The order name is Lepidoptera, which means "scaly wings." The reason for the name is that both moths and butterflies have scales on their wings and bodies. But moths and butterflies do have some differences.

Both moths and butterflies have two projections—called antennae, or "feelers"—from their heads. The antennae of butterflies are enlarged at the tips into small clubs. The antennae of moths are of different kinds, some hairlike and feathery, but they do not have clubs at the tips.

When butterflies are at rest, they hold their wings straight above them. Moths at rest usually hold their wings flat on each side of their bodies.

Butterflies fly during the day, and moths fly mostly at night. The ones you see flying among the flowers during the day are butterflies. Those you see flying around lights at night are moths.

O.P.B.

I have a pet turtle that hibernates in the winter. I went to school and asked the kids at school if turtles hibernate. They said that they don't. Is that true or false?

Theresa Bauccio
St. Louis, Missouri

You know very well what your turtle does. I suppose it just gets into a dark place and stays there. The question is whether that is really hibernation.

Zoologists have come to use the word *hibernation* in a special way. Technically, it applies to just a few animals, mostly mammals, that control their body temperature. During hibernation they lower their temperatures and turn down their body machinery.

Cold-blooded animals, those that do not control their body temperatures, can't just slow down their machinery that way. But many do go dormant, stay quiet, and maybe not eat anything for long periods. Many reptiles do that. So, if there is an argument, it is only about what the word *hibernation* really means.

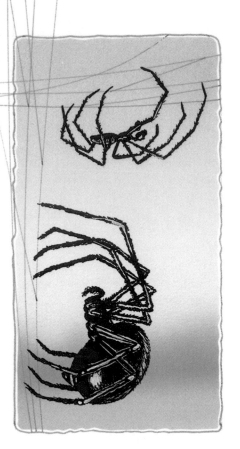

How can you tell the difference between a male and a female black widow spider?

Mindy Camls
Grand Prairie, Texas

Because George Frame recently wrote me about watching black widow spiders, I thought he could answer your question better than I could. Here is what he said.

"It isn't easy to see if a spider is a male or a female. Young spiders of both sexes look alike, but as they grow to adult size, some differences appear.

"The male black widow spider has a thinner body than does the female. The adult male black widow spider (and the male of many other kinds of spiders, too) is smaller than the adult female.

"All spiders have one pair of short 'arms' (called pedipalps) in front of their four pairs of long legs. The 'arms' of an adult male spider are always thick. Only young males and all females (young or adult) have thin 'arms.' Some people say that adult male spiders look like they are wearing boxing gloves.

"The black widow spider got its name because the adult female sometimes kills and eats her mate. If she is well fed, the male usually is not harmed."

I recently went to the zoo and saw a green polar bear. What causes it to turn green?

Aviva Pollack
San Diego, California

This happens in zoos if there are algae growing in pools of water where polar bears splash around. Some of the tiny cells of algae get into the hollow hairs of the bears and grow there. That makes the bears look green.

I think this discovery of why white polar bears become green was first made in your San Diego zoo. And it was made by a friend of mine, Dr. Ralph Lewin, who likes to look for algae growing in strange places.

As far as I can find, reports of green polar bears come only from zoos. I doubt that there are any green polar bears swimming in the Arctic Ocean.

Can you tell a male frog from a female frog? If so, how?

Becky Cable
Dallas, Texas

There is no easy way to tell a male from a female frog unless the frog is croaking or "singing." Any frog that croaks or sings is a male. Female frogs may make small sounds if they are injured or bothered, but females never sing or croak for long periods around ponds or streams, as males often do. The songs of male frogs attract the females to them during the mating season.

Another way to tell a male from a female frog is to look in the frog's mouth. Male frogs and toads have vocal sacs, or resonating chambers, that cause the songs to be louder. The openings of these vocal sacs are in the mouth, and they are in different places in frogs and toads. In common frogs, such as the leopard frog, these openings, one on each side, are in the rear part of the lower jaw near where the two jaws are hinged together. In toads, the openings to the vocal sacs are two slits in the lower jaw, one on each side of the tongue.

When male frogs and toads sing, they take air into their vocal sacs. This air causes the vocal sacs to get much bigger so that they can be seen. In frogs there are two vocal sacs, one on each side of the body. When filled with air, these sacs bulge out the body wall just behind the eye. In toads, there is one vocal sac under the lower jaw or throat. When a male toad is singing, the vocal sac sometimes gets so big that it looks like a large rounded sack to which a small toad is attached.

O.P.B.

Why do giraffes have long necks?

Lisa Marse
Metairie, Louisiana

The question *why?* is often very difficult and sometimes impossible to answer. Another question that you may be thinking about is: How did we get animals like giraffes that have such long necks?

That does seem a puzzle, and no one can tell you exactly how that happened. I have supposed that it happened this way. Way back in time, millions of years ago, there were plant-eating animals that learned to reach up in the trees for food. The higher they could reach, the better, because then they could eat juicy leaves that other animals could not reach. Taller giraffes had an advantage because they could reach higher. They had more to eat, they were stronger, and they had more babies. That meant the giraffes kept getting taller, or got longer necks, because that kind always had the advantage.

I think you can see how that could happen. Of course, I cannot prove to you that it happened this way. But no one has told me a more sensible explanation.

You will learn more about things like this as you study biology. The long neck of the giraffe is a curiosity. But almost every animal has something special or peculiar about it, and you can wonder how it got that way.

Though fleas jump, and do not fly, do they have wings?

Christa Gormley
Bloomington, Indiana

Fleas do not have wings, but they can easily get around because they are great jumpers. I think that for their size, fleas are the champion jumpers among the insects. A person who could jump as well as the best flea jumper could probably jump over the Washington Monument.

Fleas live on birds and mammals. They are a nuisance because they bite. Actually they are more than just a nuisance because they can carry diseases from one animal to another. One disease carried among rats and also from rats to people is called bubonic plague. Many years ago (especially in the years 1347 to 1351, if you like numbers) it was the worst disease in all of Europe and killed almost a third of the people. Bubonic plague is no longer as common. Today we know how the disease is carried. And good medical treatments are known.

If there are fleas in a house, they probably were brought in by pet dogs or cats. If people have fleas in a house or yard, they should ask a veterinarian how to get rid of them.

O.P.B.

Why can't rabbits make sounds?

Eric Dodson
Niles, Ohio

Actually rabbits can make sounds, but they seldom do. I do not really know why.

People who have had long experience with rabbits say that the animals sometimes make low grunting noises. They believe that the grunting noises mean that the rabbits are pleased. Also, tame rabbits will sometimes thump their hind legs on the floor of the cage. It is believed that these sounds are meant to be warnings of possible danger. People who spend a lot of time in the wild have told me that an injured or wounded rabbit will sometimes squeal or scream.

There are many different kinds of rabbits in the United States, and it may be that some kinds make more noises than others. According to one report, Indians in the northern parts of the United States and in Canada often attracted snowshoe rabbits to them by making squeaking sounds. This trick worked only during the mating season, and it may be that during this time rabbits make these sounds to attract other rabbits. I do not know if this method of attracting snowshoe rabbits is still used.

O.P.B.

Why do crickets chirp? I think they do it to put other animals to sleep. Is that true? And why at night?

Marie Aquino
West Paterson, New Jersey

I think there probably are two reasons why crickets chirp. At least in most kinds of crickets, the chirping is done by the males. The chirping is a kind of mating call and helps a female find the male. Also, it probably serves as a warning to other males to stay away.

As you say, most cricket chirping occurs at night. I cannot really say why except that most crickets seem to be nocturnal, or night-loving, animals.

Flying fish don't really fly, do they?

Jody Schmidt
DePere, Wisconsin

Flying fish are certainly among the most interesting sights that one is likely to see on an ocean voyage. Suddenly the little fish break the water surface and go sailing away like so many streaks of light.

The questions most often asked about flying fish are: how do they get out of the water, and do they actually fly?

The "wings" of the flying fish are the front fins, which are greatly enlarged. The fish gets into the air by swimming very rapidly near the water surface by strong movements of the tail. Suddenly the fish comes to the surface, spreads the front fins, and holds them rigid. The fins act like the wings of a glider; they lift the fish into the air, and keep it there as it goes sailing over the waves. Flying fish may stay in the air for several hundred yards, and sometimes they get so high that they land on the decks of large ships.

At one time it was thought that a flying fish actually flew by flapping its fins as a bird does its wings, but it is now known that the fins are held rigid and not flapped. Thus flying fish do not actually fly like birds, but they sail, or glide, like gliders.

O.P.B.

Is the platypus a mammal?

Carla Della Vedova
Brightwaters, New York

The platypus usually is considered to be a mammal because its features are like those of other mammals. For example, it has hair over most of its body and has mammary glands that make milk for its young. It also has pretty good temperature control so it can be called warm-blooded.

One characteristic, however, that is more like the reptiles is that the female lays eggs which develop outside her body.

A platypus is a water-loving animal that lives along streams in Australia. You probably have heard about it because it is partly like a reptile and partly like a mammal.

Actually, it should be no surprise that there are some animals that do not fit exactly into groups like reptiles and mammals. After all, these names just stand for man-made ideas.

I am quite sure that a platypus doesn't care whether we think it's a mammal or a reptile.

Why do fish live in pet stores but not at home? They die about two days after I get them. Why?

Robin Mirsky
Hicksville, New York

I doubt that I can tell you why. The trouble is that there are a number of possible reasons. I think the first thing to do is to go to the pet store and ask for advice. But I can tell you some of the problems you need to solve in order to keep fish as pets.

One problem with fish is to keep enough oxygen in their water. You and I get our oxygen from the air around us. Fish get oxygen from the water. Water does not hold much oxygen. So there must always be some way to keep putting oxygen into water, usually from air, to replace what the fish are using up. Cool water holds more oxygen than warm water. So usually it is best to keep fish in a cool place.

Another problem can arise from chlorine in our water. Usually it is added to our water to kill bacteria. Chlorine is not very good for fish. One way to get rid of the chlorine is to let a bowl of water stand open for a day.

Another kind of problem occurs with fish if you feed them too much. Most fish really do not need much food. Overfed fish are not likely to be healthy.

Some fish are easier to keep than others. Goldfish have been used as pets for years and years partly because they are easy to keep.

I have tried to tell you some ideas about fish that may be helpful. But my best advice is: Ask someone who already has fish and knows about how to keep them.

Do fish sleep?

Yvonne Blanchard
Kilgore, Texas

Yes, I would say that fish do sleep. Some fish actually lie on the bottom at night. Some of them even produce a gooey covering as a protection against other fish who might be looking for an easy meal. In the dark many fish have a lower rate of metabolism (their body machinery slows down), and that is much like sleep.

But there is one thing you do in your sleep that fish do not do. You close your eyes. Fish can't do that. They don't have any eyelids.

How come the goldfish in my aquarium swallow the gravel and then spit it out?

Debbie Farrall
Grand Island, Nebraska

I can think of two reasons why you might see your fish mouthing gravel. Goldfish eat a wide variety of food, especially the very tiny plants (algae) and animals that grow on the surface of pebbles and rocks. One way for a goldfish to get this goody is to pick up a pebble, scrape off the algae in its mouth, and then spit out the pebble.

There is another possible reason. Most fishes have very special routines or rituals that they use in courtship. One of these is nipping at the surface of things about them. If a fish were nipping at the gravel bottom of an aquarium, it would seem to be picking up pebbles and spitting them out again. So a male goldfish behaving this way might not be eating at all but only trying to impress a female goldfish nearby—or vice versa.

C.H.

Since male deer shed their horns, how come you rarely find the horns in the woods?

*Annie Reeves
Jeddo, Michigan*

I have wondered about that, too. I decided to ask a young friend, Scott Wendlandt, who has spent a lot of time watching and studying deer. Here is what he told me:

First, you must consider that deer range over rather wide areas, maybe twenty acres or more. Just to find a set of antlers within twenty acres, even when the antlers are first shed, would take careful searching and some luck. A second reason is that such rodents as squirrels and rats like to chew on antlers, perhaps because of the calcium or phosphate that they contain.

Scott says that he has found only about twenty cast-off antlers, even after years of looking for them. And most of those were partly chewed up. It's interesting to realize that even deer horns are recycled in nature.

Why do rabbits jump instead of just running away?

*Denise Saucier
Uxbridge, Massachusetts*

You are right that rabbits have a special way of moving around. They go in jumps or hops one after the other.

Rabbits have long and strong back legs. They take off on a hop with a big push from their back legs. They land on their front legs and then bring the back legs forward to get ready for another hop.

If you were built like a rabbit, I think you might travel that way, too.

About two days ago a deer was by my house. He was so tame you could pet him. The conservation department told us he was only eight months old. Much construction is taking away the homes of wildlife. Can you tell me if I can help?

Kelly Rozewicz
Cheektowaga, New York

Kelly, I understand and worry about that, too. The places where your home is and where my home is were once part of wild America. There are more and more people on this earth, and we take up more and more space. That leaves less and less for other animals. But we really shouldn't get mad at people who build new houses just because our houses were built first.

I don't know any way to solve the problem except to do everything we can to set aside areas for wildlife. Some animals learn to live with people better than others do. Raccoons and deer seem able to get along pretty well. Of course, deer don't get along well in the cities. But in spite of all the new construction, there are many more deer in New York State now than there were one hundred years ago.

I think we all need to understand the problem and then do whatever we can.

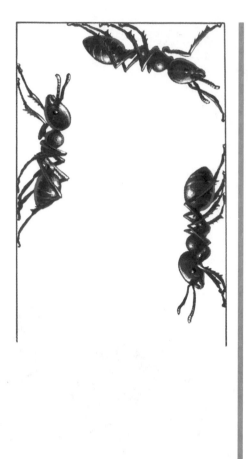

I would like to know why ants can carry so much when there are very few people who can carry even one hundred pounds?

*Kelly Jones
Denver, Colorado*

It is true that most insects, including ants, are comparatively stronger than people. By using a special kind of machine, it has been found that the average insect can pull about twenty times its weight. On this same kind of machine, a man cannot even pull his own weight.

An ant can lift more than fifty times its weight with its teeth, and a beetle has lifted several hundred times its weight on its back. If a man could do as well, he could lift almost four tons with his teeth, and carry more than sixty tons on his back. If a man could jump as well as a flea, compared to size, he could jump the length of several football fields, and more than four hundred feet high. A man would not want to jump this far or this high. He would splatter all over the ground when he landed.

There are several reasons that insects are so strong. One is their small size. A small animal is comparatively stronger than a large animal. If an insect were as large as a man, it would not be nearly so strong compared to its size. Another reason insects are so strong is the way insect muscles work differently and better than the muscles of people.

How do ants walk on the ceiling without falling off?

*Kevin Clough
Oak Forest, Illinois*

I haven't been able to find an answer in any books, so I asked my friend, Larry Gilbert, who is an entomologist studying insects. He is not sure, but he thinks that many insects have tiny bristles or short hairs on the bottoms of their feet. If that's true, the hairs must be tiny—small enough to hold on to very small irregularities in the surface.

Some insects, maybe ants, can walk on the underside of glass. Of course, even glass has a rough surface when seen by a powerful microscope.

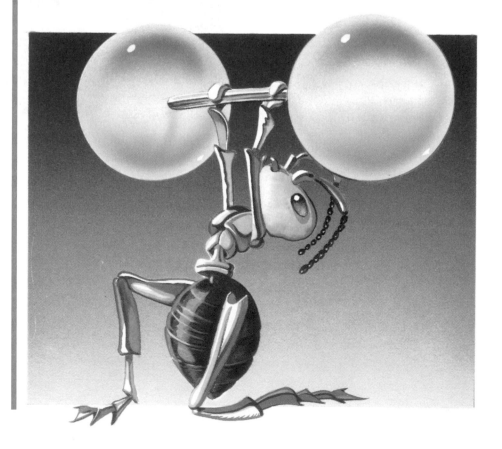

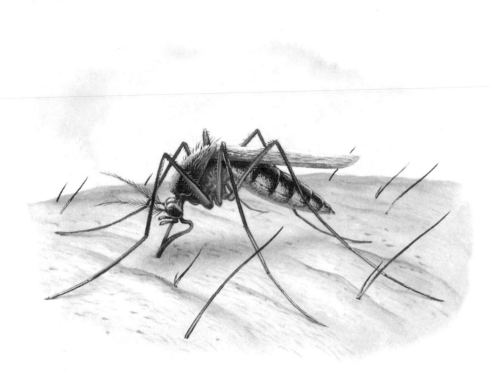

I have tons of mosquito bites. They are driving me crazy. Why do mosquito bites itch?

Laura Monick
North Tonawanda, New York

When a female mosquito sticks her beak into your skin to get a meal of blood, she leaves a little of her saliva in the wound. I guess almost all humans are allergic to something in mosquito saliva. So, we get an allergic reaction, and the skin around the bite itches and gets red.

Why do ladybugs (or ladybirds) have dots? We have a collection of them and have been looking in books and encyclopedias for the answer. We hope you know.

Judith and Donna Stasmey
Normal, Illinois

If you have been making a collection of ladybugs, I think you must know more about them than I do. (I had to do some looking up in books, too.)

I think you already know that ladybugs are small beetles, that they belong to the family of insects called the Coccinellidae, and that they are helpful to farmers because their larvae eat aphids.

It seems that ladybird beetles (as they are also called) live all over the world. And there are supposed to be about 350 different kinds or species in the United States.

I don't even know whether all kinds of ladybird beetles have spots, and I would not be sure that it was a ladybird if it did not.

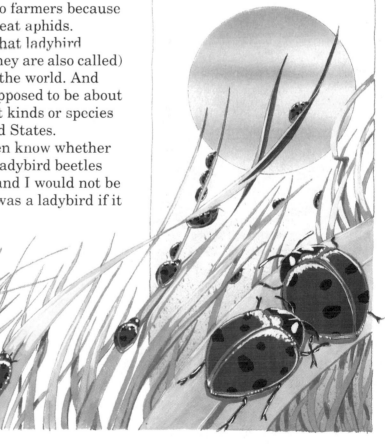

I have a dog and a cat that seem as if they are always communicating. I want to know how this is done.

Jenny Rudd
Jeffersonville, Indiana

If you carefully watch your dog and cat, I think you will learn the answer. I think you will find that they use what we call body language. People use this all the time, even though we also have a language of words.

People frown or scowl or grin, sometimes hunch their shoulders, and make gestures with their hands. If you think about this idea and then watch your cat and dog, I think you will see that they use body language, too.

Do cats really have nine lives?

Shawna Clark
Michigan City, Indiana

I guess both of us have heard that saying many times. We don't really believe it, but there must be a reason for the saying. There is.

You and other animals have a reflex that helps you stay balanced. It is called the **righting reflex.** This works so neatly that you may not have noticed it. A time to feel it happen is when you are walking and your foot slips. Then a number of muscles in your legs, your back, maybe even your shoulders suddenly work to try to keep your body upright.

Cats are world champions in having a well-developed righting reflex. If a cat starts to fall out of a tree, it twists its whole body in midair and lands on its feet. So, cats often survive falls that would kill most animals. I think that's where the idea came from that cats may have more than one life.

What I cannot answer is where the *nine* comes from. It might mean that a cat will survive a bad fall nine out of ten times. Or maybe nine is just a nice number. Or maybe you can think of a better reason.

I have a cat. It's all black. My question is, at nighttime when it is a full moon, why do my cat's eyes light up?

Nicole Robinson
Baltimore, Maryland

The eyes of other animals are very much like yours. Light gets in through the pupil, the little dark spot in the center, and is focused by the lens to make a small picture on the retina. The retina is a filmy layer of light-sensitive nerve cells at the back of the eye. In most animal eyes the retina is supported by a dark-colored layer just behind it. The dark layer absorbs any light that gets through the retina. So, the pupil of the eye looks black because very little light ever gets back out.

Some animals are nocturnal, meaning that they are active at night. And some of the nocturnal animals have eyes with a special feature. Instead of a dark layer behind the retina, they have a shiny reflecting layer called the **tapetum**. That seems like a good way for helping an eye to see in very dim light. We suppose that reflection by the tapetum doubles the chance that a light ray will fall on a light-sensitive cell of the retina.

Now we can answer your question. An eye with a tapetum also does a special trick. Some of the light that enters the pupil goes right back out the way it came in. So if you are out in the woods at night with a flashlight, the eyes of a cat or a raccoon or an alligator seem to shine right back at you.

I have a cat named Puff. One day she was sitting in my bedroom window. I could see Puff's reflection in the glass. Could she see her reflection?

Carrie Lancaster
Wagoner, Oklahoma

I think the answer is yes. Animals can see their reflections just as you and I can. Your cat, Puff, must even know that the reflection she sees is her own and is not another cat.

A cardinal that lives in my yard is not so smart. Often he comes to my bedroom window very early in the morning and wakes me up by pecking against the window. He seems to be fighting his reflection as if it were another cardinal moving into his territory.

Why do cats always arch their backs and hiss when they are alarmed?

Mary McGuire
Penns Neck, New Jersey

I didn't know the answer to your question, so I asked Lory Frame for help. Lory, who is a naturalist, has written many articles about animals. Here is what she had to say:

When a cat arches its back and hisses, it feels it is facing a dangerous enemy. In most cases the cat is not eager to fight. It would rather just escape. So it pulls itself up to look big and frightening enough to make the enemy think twice. That's when the cat gets the chance to run away.

As for hissing, that's a threat, too. Mother cats defend their babies by hissing at intruders, and sometimes they even hiss at their own kittens. This sends them scurrying

back to the nest. The hiss is so alarming that the kittens learn to be more cautious when that particular enemy appears again.

Many animals hiss as a way of scaring each other. I have seen vultures in Africa threaten each other during squabbles over food by spreading their wings and hissing. This makes them appear bigger and more frightening. And once, when I was little and visiting my grandmother, a big white goose of hers hissed at me when I peeked inside the coop to look at her nest full of eggs. Did I ever jump!

When animals are frightened or want an enemy to back off, they may try to appear more dangerous than they really feel. But there is something we should remember: If a frightened animal is cornered or pushed too far, it will use whatever weapons it has to defend itself. In the case of cats, the weapons are sharp teeth and claws. Many dogs and people have discovered that.

My dog M.J. had five puppies. I think she mated with five dogs. Do you know why? She had a white pup with black spots, two brown pups, a black one with white spots, and a brown one with white spots.

P.S. Their names are Marble, Penny, Spots, Pacific, and Mercury.

Paula Scheerer
Pasadena, Maryland

Different-color puppies are not really so unusual. I think that all of them may well be full brothers and sisters. Differences in color are only differences in pigment in the skin, "only skin deep," and not really very important. You can easily see differences among human brothers and sisters in hair color, eye color, and just how they look. In fact, that's common in most animals.

You may be thinking of dogs that have been "pure bred," such as collies. Collies look like collies because they've been "selected" for hundreds of years. If collies are always mated to collies, then their puppies look like collies and have almost the same coloration.

But if dogs are not purebred, then their puppies may have the same variations that we see in many wild animals.

I hope you still like your puppies.

I have a dog that whines when I play the harmonica. Is she crying or singing?

Stacy Hickey
Poughkeepsie, New York

I did not know the answer to your question, so I sent it to our friend Dr. John J. Mettler. Dr. Mettler is a veterinarian. Here is what Dr. Mettler said about your question:

It is not uncommon for dogs to try to imitate sounds they hear. For instance, some dogs howl when they hear a fire siren, and a boy I knew had a dog that used to sing when the boy played the violin. If a dog hears a sound it doesn't like, it will run and hide, so I expect the dog is singing.

Why don't birds get shocked when they sit on wires?

Sajan Eapen
Houston, Texas

That does look surprising. Birds sometimes sit on wires carrying thousands of volts and held up high by big towers.

Living things, like birds and people, can get shocked by touching two different wires or touching one wire and the ground. Then electricity has a way in and out, and can flow through a body and give a dangerous shock.

For example, you will notice that the cord to an electric lamp or an electric motor always has at least two wires to carry electricity in and out.

A bird on an electric wire is safe and happy—unless it makes the mistake of touching another wire at the same time. Then it's a dead bird.

How come owls have very big eyes?

Sharona Shotkin
Patchogue, New York

The eyes of owls are different from those of most birds. They are large, and both eyes are located on the front side of the head.

If you watch birds, you will notice that most of them have their eyes located on the sides of their heads. They can look at something with one eye at a time. This helps them look for food on the ground. And it makes it easier for the bird to see a cat that might be sneaking up on one side.

Because its eyes are in front, an owl cannot see to one side without turning its head. But it can use both eyes together, the way you do, to help judge distance to whatever it is looking at.

How do birds lose their feathers and then grow back their feathers so they are not bald?

Debra Suerstonas
Thomaston, Connecticut

Feathers are remarkable gadgets. I am sure that if anyone could find a way to build anything as strong and yet as light, they would wish to patent the process.

Feathers are made from a hardened protein, called keratin, about the same kind of stuff that you use to make hair and fingernails.

The feathers you see on a bird do not contain any living cells. But each one is made by a collection of cells in a little pocket or follicle in the skin. A bird has several different kinds of feathers and each follicle can produce only one kind. The follicles are lined up on the skin to make a pattern which is special for each kind of bird.

Since feathers contain no living cells, they cannot be repaired when they get broken or worn. So most birds have a regular schedule of replacing feathers once or twice a year. In molting, an old feather slips out of its attachment and a follicle starts building a new feather. Most birds replace their long flight feathers only a few at a time, which seems a sensible way to go about it.

I guess the answer to your question is that birds do not get bald because their follicles keep working to make new feathers.

We humans have hair instead of feathers. Hair is nice. Losing it and being bald is an inconvenience (as I know very well). But for a bird, being bald would be a catastrophe. I am sure you can see why.

When a bird flies, why don't its wings get tired?

Rayna Polsky
New Britain, Pennsylvania

No one really knows whether a bird gets tired flying. I suspect that sometimes they do.

Birds that are in the air most of the time—or those that fly long distances in migration—fly rather slowly. A muscle that works steadily and slowly can be made to work without getting tired. (Think about your heart muscle.)

Some birds, especially larger ones, spend a lot of time soaring on air currents. They don't need to flap their wings when they soar. You have noticed that many birds do not fly all the time. Most of them, such as the ones around my bird feeder, seem to do a lot of resting.

Was Brontosaurus really afraid of Allosaurus? Was Triceratops afraid of anything?

Scott Carlson
Elk Grove, Illinois

Everything we can say about dinosaurs comes from studying fossil remains. Teeth tell about what the animal ate. The shape and size of bones tell about the animal's size and strength. And tracks preserved in the rock tell about how an animal walked. By comparing fossil teeth and bones with those of other animals, we get ideas about how an animal looked.

Brontosaurus is pictured as a very large, blimplike, plant-eating animal. Just from its jaws and teeth we know that Allosaurus must have been a meat-eater. No one will ever know what a Brontosaurus thought about. Its skull had room for only a very small brain, so it could not have done much thinking.

However, I can say that if I had been a Brontosaurus I surely would have been afraid of that vicious-looking Allosaurus.

Triceratops got its name from its three sharp horns. These stuck out of a big bony shield that protected it in front. Sometimes it is compared to today's rhinoceros. If I had been a Triceratops, I think I wouldn't have been afraid, except maybe of a bigger Triceratops.

If a paleontologist finds a fossil, he will know how long ago it came from. How does he know?

Jordy Moldofsky
Toronto, Ontario

I asked my friend Jack Wilson to answer your question. He is a paleontologist. Here is what he said:

Telling particular kinds of animals apart is no different than telling different makes of automobiles apart.

A paleontologist is a person who has studied fossil animals enough so that he can tell the bones of one animal from another. Like the differences between cars, there are differences that he looks for to help him identify bones.

Telling the age during which an animal lived is like trying to learn the year a car was made without the auto company records. The paleontologist has three clues. First, all fossils are found in rocks, and those rocks and fossils that are on the bottom are oldest. By fitting together stacks of rock and fossils from various places, he works out ages in terms of older-than or younger-than.

Secondly, animals, like cars, have changed with time. Generally the older ones are simpler and the newer ones are more complex. The third clue sometimes is available if the fossil bones are found with certain minerals which are radioactive. These minerals can be analyzed in a way that tells how old they are.

I was wondering if dinosaurs had trunks like elephants. At the Melbourne Museum there was an exhibition of dinosaur fossils. Near the Mamenchisaurus was a skeleton of an adult elephant, and there were no bones where the trunk would be. How do scientists know that the dinosaurs in the flesh had no trunks?

Sunil Daniel
Bendigo, Australia

I see what you mean. Fossils are made from the bones of an animal's skeleton, not from the muscles and soft parts of its body.

If you look again at an elephant skeleton in the museum, you should notice the large nasal bones about the mouth. If these have been preserved on the skeleton, you will see that they are just right for attaching a trunk.

Something that is as big and heavy as an elephant's trunk needs a good strong bone for its attachment to the skull.

A human skull or a dinosaur skull has a nasal bone that is enough to support a nose sticking out in front, but not a long trunk. So you can tell from the fossils that humans and dinosaurs never had trunks.

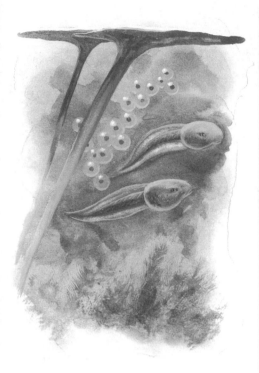

Can frogs breathe underwater?

Jonathan Phipps
Tatla Lake, British Columbia

The answer is yes, but I need to say something more.

A frog has two ways of breathing. It can breathe air into its lungs much as you do. It also can do some of its breathing through its skin. That means it can get some oxygen from the water around it and get rid of carbon dioxide, too.

When you scare a frog sitting at the edge of a pond, it takes a big gulp of air as it dives in. The frog is not very active underwater and doesn't need to breathe very fast. So, once the big gulp of air is used up, the frog continues to breathe through its skin. That works all right if the water is cool, but it doesn't work so well if the water is warm. Warm water doesn't hold as much oxygen. And warm water speeds up the frog's metabolism so it needs more oxygen. Soon it will come out for a real breath of air.

I want to know what tadpoles eat. I've got tadpoles in an aquarium, and they always stay in the gravel you use when you have fish. Why?

Billy Saylor
Mokena, Illinois

I think that tadpoles feed mostly on algae and other plants growing in the water and maybe also on small pieces of dead animal material. As you must have noticed, they can swim, but they often spend a lot of time resting and attached to something. Maybe that is why they stay mostly in the gravel.

I hope you were successful in raising some of your tadpoles and able to watch them change into little frogs.

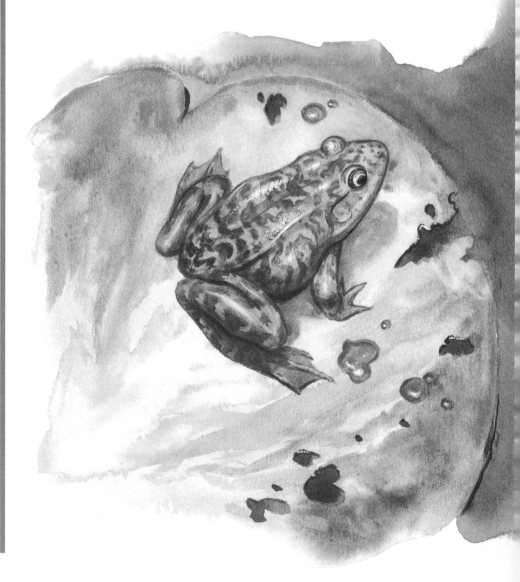

My friend has a toad. I asked my dad if you could get warts from it, but he didn't know. Is it true?

Angie Lucey
Janesville, Wisconsin

I know that some toads are warty-looking animals. But I think they are safe. I can't find that anyone ever got warts from a toad. So I think you can even try petting your friend's toad, if it looks cuddly enough.

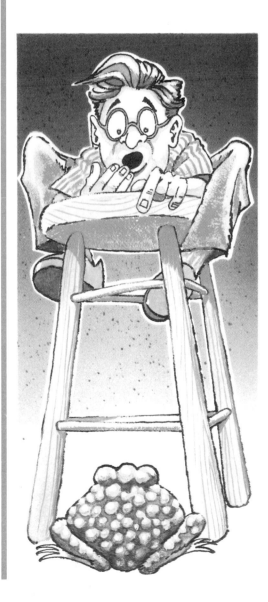

What is the difference between a frog and a toad?

David Dion
Framingham, Massachusetts

Toads and frogs are amphibians and need to live in water at least during part of their lives. But toads are able to spend much of their lives on dry land, while most frogs stay closer to water.

Toads differ from frogs in other ways, too. Toads usually have shorter hind legs and are not as good at hopping, and their skins are often dry and warty-looking.

Are killer whales really mean?

Ashley Katen
Glenrock, Wyoming

Killer whales are sometimes called the "wolves of the sea." They are predators—they need to eat other animals to make a living. And, like wolves, they work together in groups.

If you're a porpoise or a big fish, I suppose a killer whale looks pretty mean because it wants to eat you. If you're a killer whale, then you hope that the porpoise or big fish doesn't get away—because then you would have to go hungry.

After you've thought about this you can decide on an answer to your question.

Do piranhas and sharks really eat people, or do they just bite and then swim away?

Soo Mie Kwon
Belleview, Missouri

Sharks and piranhas do not feed on people very often, but both have been known to eat people. They go about this in different ways.

Of the many kinds of sharks in the ocean, a few are considered dangerous because of attacks on people. A large shark could easily eat a person and a few have been known to do this. When a shark attacks a person or an animal, it often swims by rapidly and takes a bite as it passes. After eating the bite, the shark usually returns. Sometimes sharks may go away after biting a few times, but the person or animal is usually severely injured, especially if the shark is a large one. Sometimes more than one shark will attack an animal or person.

Piranhas are much smaller than sharks, and they live in some of the rivers in South America. There are several kinds of piranhas that are several inches to a foot or so in length. A single piranha is much too small to eat a person.

However, hundreds of these little fish travel together in groups or schools. When a school of piranhas attacks a person or other animal, each fish takes a bite as it swims by. Then each fish comes back for more.

If the school is a large one, this may continue until only the animal's skeleton remains. A large school of piranhas is not at all likely to just bite and then go away.

O.P.B.

Do whales really spit water?

Megan Wolf
Fairport, New York

I think you are asking about the whale spouts or water spouts that whales make when they come to the surface. If you are, then the answer is no.

Most kinds of whales have their nostrils (like your nose) on top of their heads. When they come to the surface after a dive they want to get some fresh air. (As you probably know, they are air breathers like you and me and not gill breathers like fishes.)

Before whales can take in a breath of fresh air, they need to breathe out the old air from their lungs. They do this in a big whoosh. All that warm air has lots of water vapor that condenses out as water droplets and may also carry a little sea water along. That makes a water "spout" that may be seen for miles so that whale watchers can say, "Thar she blows."

I would like to know why dogs pant when they are not tired.

Colin McClelland
Buena Vista, Colorado

The answer is that dogs sometimes pant just to help cool off.

When your body temperature gets too high, you sweat. Evaporation of water takes up a lot of heat. Evaporation of sweat from your skin helps cool your body when its temperature begins to get too high.

Dogs (and cats, too) are pretty well covered with hair and have very little bare skin. They can't keep cool by sweating—except maybe a little from the pads of their feet. Instead, a dog pants. That moves air rapidly back and forth over the moist tissues of its mouth and tongue.

Panting is the dog's way of evaporating extra water to help keep its body cool.

I have had two dogs in my life and have seen lots, too. But the thing I'm lost about is: How do they bark?

Carrie O'Donnell
Ariss, Ontario

I guess I really do not know either. I can only tell you something about it. If you watch a dog, you will see that its ribs and chest get smaller very quickly to make the bark. That means that it is driving air out of its lungs and up through its windpipe and mouth. That's also what you do if you suddenly shout, "Hey."

I think a dog's bark is like your shout. What I do not know is why a bark sounds like a bark. I suppose the special sound, just like one of yours, is made by a dog's vocal cords.

My cat can see in the dark. How?

Stacy Peterson
Two Rivers, Wisconsin

In really and truly complete darkness no animal can see. Our eyes and those of other animals see only by light rays that come to them. However, there are not many places in nature where there is complete darkness with no light rays at all. Even on a dark night there is a little light from the stars that gets through clouds.

Our eyes are good at seeing with just a little light. Some animals that hunt at night are much better. Cats and owls can see when there is so little light that you would say it was completely dark. I think that's what people mean when they say that a cat can see in the dark.

Is a dog's tail a voluntary or involuntary muscle? This has been puzzling me for a long time.

Elaine Stensbol
La Habra, California

A dog's tail must be moved by a voluntary muscle. As you know, a voluntary muscle is one you can control from the brain. An involuntary muscle is one which you cannot control by thinking about it—like the muscle in your heart.

I see why you might ask the question. A dog wags his tail as if that were an automatic response when he is pleased. There are many kinds of animal (and human) behavior like that. You can pretty well count on a person smiling or laughing if he is pleased, or crying if he is hurt or very sad. The muscles that do those things are voluntary muscles, but they often work together in some special pattern.

Each kind of animal has its own special patterns of behavior. Tail wagging is a special pattern of dog behavior.

43

I read in many stories that elephants are afraid of mice. Is it true?

Donna Delattre
Ayer, Massachusetts

At one time many people thought elephants were afraid of mice. It was believed the reason for this fear was that the mouse might get into the end of the elephant's trunk. The idea was that the mouse might scratch the lining of the trunk or plug up the trunk so the elephant could not breathe.

It is now known that none of these beliefs are true. In zoos, mice have been seen running about very near the tip of an elephant's trunk, and the elephant did not pay any attention to them.

Elephants have a very keen sense of smell, and they depend on this to warn them of danger. They may not be able to see mice on the floor, but they certainly can smell them as the mice scamper about near the tips of their trunks.

The hole at the end of an elephant's trunk would be a strange hole for a mouse. I do not believe a mouse would run into this strange hole without looking in first. By the time the mouse could have looked into the end of the trunk, the elephant would have smelled it. The elephant could then "snort" and blow out a little air which should keep the mouse out of the trunk.

It may be that a mouse has gotten into an elephant's trunk at one time or another. If so, I have never heard or read of it. In fact, I cannot imagine why a mouse would want to get into an elephant's trunk!

O.P.B.

How do snakes hear?

Kristi Wilson
Memphis, Tennessee

Snakes do not have ears outside the head as we do, nor do they have ear openings or eardrums. We have parts of our hearing apparatus, called the inner ear, inside the head, and snakes have these parts also.

When a person or animal walks, it makes vibrations which pass through the earth to the body of the snake. It has been known for a long time that snakes can feel vibrations from the ground. The vibrations pass through the skin and muscles of the snake to a bone connected to its inner ear. From this bone, the vibrations pass to the inner ear, which "hears" them.

It is now known that snakes can also hear noises or vibrations that travel through the air. The vibrations caused by noises are also called sound waves. When people and most animals hear, sound waves strike the eardrum and go to the inner ear, which is sensitive to the sound waves or vibrations. Snakes do not have eardrums, but their skins, muscles, and bones carry the sound waves to the inner ears. In this way snakes can hear sound carried by the air, but probably not so well as we can.

What is it that makes some snakes poisonous?

Ashlee Gray
Marietta, Georgia

Some snakes are venomous. They have little needlelike fangs that inject a milky fluid when the snakes bite. The fluid is called a venom because it contains poisons. Since I didn't know what the poisons are, I had to do some reading. I was surprised to discover that there are whole books written about snake venoms.

There are different kinds of venomous snakes. Their venoms are not all alike, but they have some common features. Almost all of their chemicals are special proteins, not just one but a number of different kinds. Some are neurotoxins, which poison nerve endings so that they cannot carry nerve messages. Some make blood clot and plug up veins so that blood cannot flow. Some cause a breakdown of the membranes around red blood cells so that the cells break up and no longer work in carrying oxygen. Some of them are enzymes that dissolve some of the gluelike stuff that holds cells together.

Snake venom helps a snake digest its food. Think of a rattlesnake that has just struck a mouse and injected some venom. The snake can't do any chewing and swallows the whole mouse. Digesting big lumps of food is a slow job. That's why you chew your food before swallowing. If the rattlesnake injects some venom into the mouse before it dies, that is a way to get enzymes all through the body of the mouse. Then the whole mouse—not just its surface—is easy for the snake to digest.

After reading about rattlesnake venom, I think I will carefully stay away from rattlesnakes.

Are horses vegetarians?

Jill Landis
St. Louis, Missouri

I asked Dr. John J. Mettler, a veterinarian, to answer your question. Here is his answer:

Yes, horses are vegetarians. When talking about animals we usually use a different word that has almost the same meaning. We could say they are herbivores. Like cows, deer, goats, sheep, and rabbits, horses eat only plants. There is another group of animals that, in nature, live on meat. Dogs, wolves, and cats such as lions, tigers, and house cats are called carnivores. Pet dogs have learned from their owners to eat foods other than meat, but for a healthy diet they do need some meat.

There are some animals, called omnivores, that eat both meat and plants. These include bears, pigs, raccoons, and humans.

You can make a good guess about whether an animal is a carnivore or herbivore by noticing how its eyes are placed. A herbivore usually has eyes on the sides of its head. That helps it see all around to watch for danger. A carnivore usually has eyes that look straight ahead. That's a good arrangement for an animal that must chase its food.

My friend says her horse is hyperactive. Can horses really be hyperactive?

Renee Hoppens
Friendswood, Texas

I think a clue to the answer to that question is: People are not all alike. Some are nervous and excitable and like to be always moving. I guess that's what you mean by hyperactive. I think some horses are, too. Some of them are said to be jittery or frisky or high-strung. I think that means about the same thing.

It is easy to see that people are not all alike, and horses are also not all alike in their behavior.

Why are baby goats called kids?

Eileen Milliken
Drexel Hill, Pennsylvania

I don't know and I doubt that we will find out. The first meaning of "kid" given in my dictionary is "baby goat." And it seems that almost that same spelling is also used in other languages. So that word and meaning must have been used for a long time.

Another, and later, meaning of "kid" is a young person—like you. I don't know how that meaning got started. Maybe because, like young goats, young people are playful animals. Does that sound OK?

Do chickens have ankles?

Alex Padilla
Cincinnati, Ohio

Your question puzzled me. I do not really know much about chickens, so I asked my friend Kathy Dodge to answer your question. Kathy lives on a small farm near us and sometimes does illustrations for HIGHLIGHTS. She has two pigs, fifteen sheep, two cows, and a large flock of chickens. Here is her answer:

I hoped my chickens could show me where their ankles were, but they couldn't. I looked in some books instead. I found out that the legs of birds are almost the same as the legs of other animals, but the part that you might think of as the ankle is called the shank (or tarsus). This is the straight thin part between the foot, claws, or toes, and the joint near the body. The rest of the bird's leg is hidden under the bird's feathers. These are the leg and the thigh, the parts you eat if you have chicken legs for supper.

So I guess we could say chickens do have ankles, but we usually only talk about the feet, shanks, legs, and thighs.

47

Someone told me that a turtle doesn't have a heartbeat. Is that true or not?

Richard Bedard
Waterbury, Connecticut

Someone told me that a turtle doesn't have a heartbeat. Is that true or not?

A turtle has a very strong heartbeat. As a matter of fact, college students often use a turtle in studying the heart and its beat.

A turtle, like other reptiles, actually has a heart built a little differently from yours. A turtle's heart has three chambers whereas yours has four. But in having a heart that keeps thumping away to pump blood, a turtle's heart works very much like yours.

How do turtles get their shells?

Andrea Lynn
Horsefly, British Columbia

The shell is part of the turtle's body, and the young turtle has the shell when it hatches from the egg. The shell develops or grows in the egg just as do other parts of the body. It grows around the turtle's body and becomes connected to the ribs and to the backbone.

The part of the shell on the back is called the carapace, and the part under the tummy is the plastron. The carapace and the plastron are connected together on each side by a bony plate. Some people believe that a turtle can crawl from its shell, but this is not true. It has no more chance of crawling from its shell than it has of going off and leaving some other part of the body.

Since a turtle has a shell, parts of its body are different from other animals. One of these differences is in the parts of the skeleton called the shoulder blades. Your shoulder blades are the flat bones on the back just behind where the arms are attached to the body. In people and other animals, the shoulder blades are outside the ribs. In turtles, the shoulder blades are inside the ribs.

Another difference is where the front legs attach to the skeleton. In turtles, this attachment is inside the ribs. In other animals the attachment is outside the ribs.

I guess it is no surprise that a turtle has to have a special arrangement of some of its bones to fit them inside its shell.

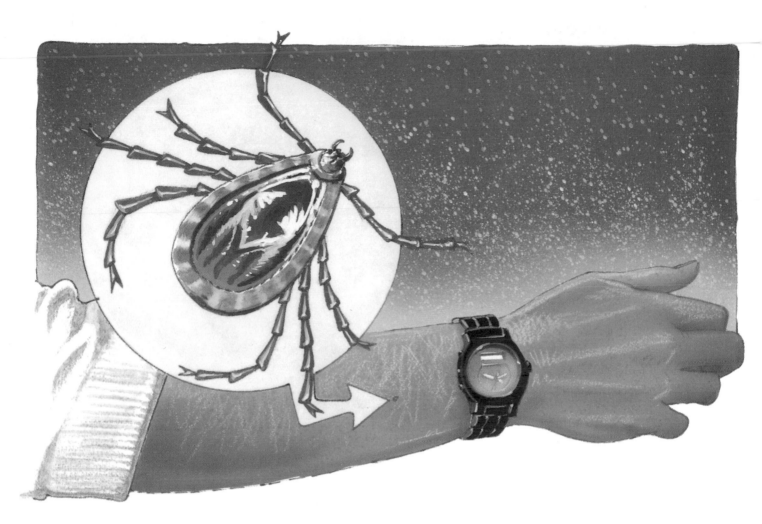

Wood ticks bother me very much. What are they good for?

Dawn Thatcher
Superior, Wisconsin

When most people ask that kind of question I think they really mean to ask, "What good are wood ticks to me as a human?" That is a question we might ask about other living things. What good is a mosquito? What good is a rattlesnake? To us as humans there are many organisms that seem to be a nuisance—or are really dangerous. And I do not know any simple way to answer that kind of question.

Many living organisms have developed and live together in the world. Each of them plays its own special role in nature. A biologist would say that each one fills an ecological niche.

As humans we are only one of the kinds of animals in nature. Because we are so smart, we have become the dominant kind of animal in the world. Maybe because we are so powerful, we are also likely to be arrogant. That leads us to think the rest of nature ought to be arranged just for us. And that leads us to look at some living things and ask what good they are to us.

We might turn your question around and ask: "Do I have a greater right than a wood tick to live on earth?" Or we might wonder: "If a wood tick could think, how would it ask the question?" It might ask: "What good are humans to me?"

I believe we should think of ourselves as a part of nature rather than that nature is made just for us. If you are willing to think of wood ticks as a part of nature, then you have answered your question.

Is the inky liquid an octopus squirts out poisonous?

*Jessica Richardson
Hopkinton, Massachusetts*

When alarmed, the octopus squirts out that cloud of inky liquid behind it. The cloud is like a smoke screen to cover its escape. The brown or black cloud is inky because it contains a lot of a common animal pigment, melanin. In fact, the original sepia ink comes from the ink sacs of cuttlefish, which are close relatives of the octopus.

The ink may also contain some chemicals which poison the smell receptors and help

discourage a predator. But I think the smoke screen effect is more important.

We went to an aquarium and saw many fish. We also saw an electric eel. How does an electric eel make electricity?

*Barbara Kurcz
Niles, Illinois*

I don't know all about electric eels but I can tell you a little about them. The first idea is that all animals (and plants, too) make some electricity. Tiny electric currents flow in a nerve fiber when it is carrying a message and in a muscle cell when it is working.

Some fishes like the electric eel specialize in making electricity. They have special muscle cells called electroplaques. These work like tiny batteries. Thousands of them are lined up lengthwise along the fish and can be discharged all at once to give a discharge of up to a thousand volts. I understand that the fish use this as a way to kill or scare away their enemies.

There are also other electric fish that can't give a big shock but can create a small electric field around them. Then they can detect anything that gets close and changes that electric field. So they have an "electric sense."

I guess the main idea is that electricity is something common in all animals on a very small scale. Some animals have become specialized to use electricity on a large scale.

Does a goldfish have any means of defense?

Lisa Koeller
Naperville, Illinois

I am not an expert on fish, but I can't think of any special means of defense that a goldfish can have. Goldfish are really special varieties of carp which have been bred in captivity for thousands of years. But even wild carp do not seem to have any special means of defense against being eaten by bigger fish.

When you said "means of defense," I suppose you were thinking about some way in which an animal can fight back if attacked. There are many animals which cannot fight back. Some of them can run or swim fast to escape, some of them hide, some of them just try to stay out of the way of possible attackers.

I have watched minnows in a lake near where I live. They have no means of defense against a hungry bass. But the bass never find all of them and there are minnows living in that lake year after year.

Do fish drink any kind of liquid?

Kelly Mitchell
Carson, California

I don't see how a big fish could swallow a minnow or a worm without getting some water, too. So I expect that any fish must drink at least some of the water around it.

Of course, it is no surprise if a freshwater fish drinks the water around him. You and I drink the same water, usually from some river or lake where fish live.

What about fish that live in the salt water of the ocean? You and I cannot drink much ocean water. It contains too much salt and would make us sick. But a saltwater fish can. In fact, he has to drink some to stay alive. Saltwater fish have a very special way of getting rid of salt through their gills.

Most freshwater fish, such as goldfish or black bass, cannot live in the ocean. They do not have that special way of getting rid of salt. So, like you and I, they can't drink salt water.

51

While studying my science, I read that cold-blooded animals must hibernate to survive cold. Why is it that bears, which are mammals and warm-blooded, need to hibernate?

Angela Sun
La Palma, California

There are many animals, even insects, that become dormant or inactive and hide away during the winter. I guess most people would say that such animals are hibernating.

Some zoologists, the scientists who study animals, have become very fussy about what should be called hibernation. The idea is that true hibernation is something special. It occurs only in warm-blooded animals, in fact, I think only in bats and in rodents such as the woodchucks and ground squirrels.

In hibernation the animal seems to be almost dead. Besides being asleep, it has a much-lowered body temperature, a lowered heart rate, and a lowered breathing rate. And it is so asleep that it warms up and wakes up very slowly. For true hibernation an animal's body machinery must be turned down until it is just barely alive, and then its machinery must be turned up again to wake it up.

It was a surprise to me to discover that bears do not have true hibernation. Of course, they hole up in a den for a winter sleep. But they may wake up many times during the winter. And they wake up more easily than true hibernators do. In fact, if you should find a sleeping bear during the winter, it is not a good idea to kick it.

Cold-blooded animals do not hibernate, simply because they have no control of their body temperature at all. Getting cold just turns them off until they warm up again in the spring. So what about a frog that spends the winter burrowed in the mud of a pond? I guess you should say that it is dormant.

Now that I have said all this, I should also say that not everyone uses the word hibernation in the same way. I have decided that it is best not to correct anyone or to get into arguments about it. Just understanding what people mean usually is good enough. That's what language is for.

Why do animals have fur?

Suzanne Spoelhof
Jenison, Michigan

Every animal needs a protective layer on its outside. Some animals like beetles and crabs and turtles have hard shell layers on their outsides. Most other animals have a protective layer of skin.

For most of the warm-blooded animals skin is not enough to help them keep warm. Birds have feathers and mammals have hair. Some mammals have hairs that are tightly packed and cover most of their bodies. I guess you would call that fur. That helps keep them warm.

Humans don't have much hair, except usually on top of the head. So we wear clothes. Maybe that's better than fur all over our bodies. It's easy to put on more clothes to stay warm or to take off some clothes to stay cool.

I would like to know the reason that animals can stand cold weather better than a person can.

Cindy Pepin
North Sterling, Connecticut

Of course there are many animals which cannot stand cold as well as a human. Most of the animals living in the tropics would never make it through a snowy winter, even if they could find enough to eat.

I suppose you are thinking about arctic animals like the polar bear and walrus. Their bodies are built for living in the cold. On the outside they have a thick fur or a layer of fat which helps to hold their heat inside. I suspect that their body machinery is arranged better to help conserve their body heat. And many of the arctic animals have special habits of living which help, too.

There are few places in North America where humans could live all winter without any clothes or houses to keep warm. Our skin is thin and not much of a cover. But we have learned how to protect ourselves and live in hot deserts, on the polar ice caps, on the floor of the ocean, and even out in space.

Can you think of any other animal which can live in so many different kinds of places as the human? It is very unlikely that any other animal ever stepped on the surface of the moon before a human named Neil Armstrong.

Where were dinosaurs first discovered and how did they get their name?

Christine Albaugh
Weston, Michigan

There is a reason that your questions are hard to answer: When dinosaur fossils were first discovered no one knew what they were. And it took some time to get used to this idea that there were animals long ago which became extinct without ever being seen by people.

One account I have read tells about fossil jaws that were discovered in a chalk quarry in Holland about 1770. They were first thought to be the jaws of a gigantic lizard. Later an Englishman by the name of Conybeare gave the animal (whatever it was) the name Mosasaurus. Once people began looking, a number of other fossil animals were found.

In 1841 Richard Owen decided that this whole group of animals, mostly very large, almost but not quite like lizards, ought to have a name. He called them the dinosaurs.

That's the best story I can find to answer your question.

I would like to know how many dinosaurs there were in the old days.

Stuart Pelle
Mapleton, Illinois

There is no way to get a very certain answer to your question. The dinosaurs lived during a long period of geologic time that lasted more than one hundred million years. That period is called the Mesozoic. Geologists usually say that the Mesozoic period ended about sixty-five million years ago. So you see, dinosaurs lived on earth during a long period of the earth's history. And not all the different kinds lived at the same time.

I found a partial answer in a recent article. A scientist who studies dinosaurs thought about the question. He counted all the different kinds of fossil dinosaurs that have been discovered: 285 kinds in the last 150 years. Recently scientists have been digging up about six new kinds every year. But you can see that our rate of making new discoveries will slow down as we get closer to finding all of them. So he estimated that there must have been about 1,000 different kinds.

If you want to be a dinosaur hunter, it's good to know that there are still hundreds of kinds waiting to be discovered.

When scientists find dinosaur bones, how do they know what bones belong to which dinosaur?

Kim Shively
Dayton, Ohio

I have never worked on fossils, but I have a friend and neighbor who does. Sometimes my children (when they were younger) would find a skull or some bones and ask me what kind of animal they came from. Usually I did not know, but my friend could tell them right away.

When they asked him how he could tell, he would answer them something like this: Suppose you found an old fender or bumper or windshield of a car. If you took it to a mechanic, he could tell you just what make of car it belonged to. Figuring out what bones belong to what kind of animal is something like figuring out that some particular shape of a fender belongs to some particular make of car.

Of course, figuring out how to fit fossil bones of dinosaurs together is tougher because no person ever saw a live dinosaur. But if you study enough dinosaur bones, you can figure out which ones must have fitted together.

I just got some rabbits. How long do rabbits live if they're in a cage? And how many days shouldn't you touch a newborn rabbit?

Justin Taylor
Sioux City, Iowa

The best place to find precise answers to your questions is from a pet store owner or a handbook on rabbit care. Your librarian will help you locate the handbook. Ideally, however, you should return to wherever you bought your rabbit and ask the store owner or pet breeder to share his knowledge with you.

Although I can't give you exact answers, I can tell you that a caged rabbit will enjoy a longer life if it's given good care, frequent attention, and even brief "vacations" in a fenced yard during warmer months. Be sure to supplement the animal's diet with fresh grass and other greens.

A good rule of thumb to follow regarding newborn bunnies is to leave them in the care of their mother until they begin to hop around on their own and leave the nest. At that point they're ready for all the love you can give them.

My hamster's eyes turn blue at night. He doesn't act sick, but his eyes are usually black. Do you think there's anything wrong with him?

Sara Blackwell
San Anselmo, California

I suppose that your hamster always looks OK the next morning. If that is true then his blue eye color at night must have some other explanation.

I have never looked into a hamster's eyes in dim light as at night. I expect that its eyes will seem to glow a little like those of other animals. The glow is called eyeshine. It comes from light reflected by a reflecting layer at the back of the eye. And it usually is colored a little by the reflecting layer.

At night a cat's eyes seem greenish, a raccoon's eyes are yellow. Maybe you have discovered that a hamster's eyeshine is blue. Do you think this might be the explanation?

Why do wolves, coyotes, and dogs howl at a full moon?

Justyna Piasecka
Washington, D.C.

I have never seen a very satisfying explanation of that question. In fact, I'm not sure just why they howl at all. Of course, wolves in the wild hunt in packs. So howling might be a way of telling each other where they are.

I can't think of a good reason why a full moon would make any difference. I wonder if that part is really true. Maybe it's just an idea that people talk about but don't bother to see if it is true.

If you find a better answer to your question, please let me know.

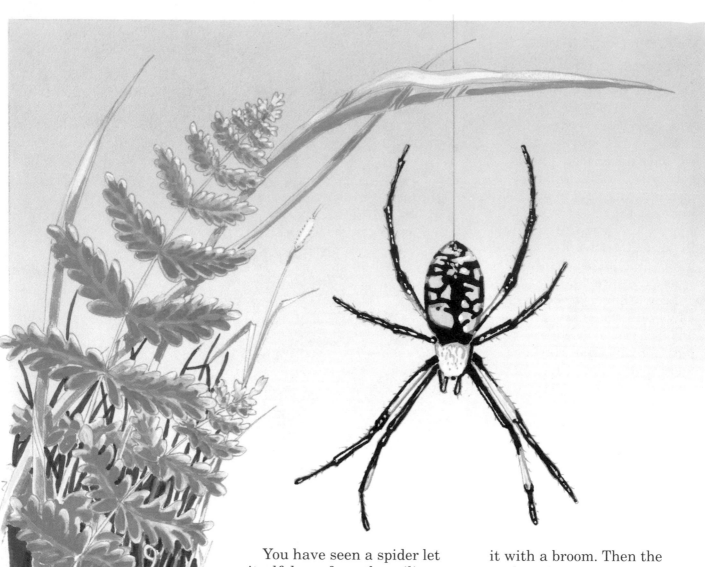

I have a puzzling question: A spider is hanging on his web from the ceiling. If you touch him, he will go up. But what happens to his web? Does he gather it up as he goes back to the ceiling, or what happens to it?

Nancy Stearns
Oakland, Oregon

You have seen a spider let itself down from the ceiling on a strand of silk and then scramble back up again. As it climbs, it catches the strand on one of its legs and rolls the silk into a ball. When the spider reaches a safe place, it will drop the ball of silk, or may even eat the silk if it is hungry.

A single strand of silk by which a spider suspends itself is called a dragline. As the spider wanders about, it pays out the dragline behind, and every once in a while attaches the line to the surface.

Sometimes the spider will deliberately jump off into space, or it may jump because an irate house cleaner punches it with a broom. Then the anchored dragline holds the spider. The spider may climb back to its former perch, or it may lower itself farther until it gets to another surface.

Spider silk, of which there are several kinds, is secreted from glands within the spider's body. The silk comes out through one or several finger-like structures called spinnerets located on the under surface of the body and toward the rear end. The silk comes from the body as a liquid but quickly hardens.

Spider silk for its size is among the strongest materials known. It is stronger than a steel wire of the same size.

I would like to know the meaning of the firefly's glow.

Salvatore Mangano
Flushing, New York

Maybe you already know that many living things can make light by a chemical reaction in their bodies. Light made this way is called bioluminescence. We know a lot about the special chemical reaction. But we do not know all about how it makes light.

In the firefly all the bioluminescence occurs at the end of the abdomen, so it might be called a tail light. The firefly can turn that light on and off to make a signal. In the evening the flashing lights you may see from fireflies come mostly from flying males. The females are more likely to be resting. When a female sees a flash from a male close by, she responds with a flash of her own.

Fireflies use their glow as the special means of signaling between males and females.

Can you tell me what fireflies eat and how to make a zoo with them?

Cheng-Jil Chen
Bayside, New York

Fireflies are not flies at all,

but they are kinds of beetles. They are also called lightning bugs. Firefly eggs hatch into little wormlike creatures called larvae. Some kinds of larvae glow in the dark, and those that do are called glow-worms. The glowworms eat very small creatures such as other insects, snails, and slugs. Some adult fireflies also eat other insects. Some eat pollen and other flower parts, and some probably do not eat anything at all.

It would be very hard to make a firefly zoo because, so far as I know, no one has been able to raise fireflies in captivity. But it is fun to capture several of them and watch them make their lights. The light of each firefly blinks on and off, but if there are several in a jar, some of their lights will be flashing most of the time.

I have a newt. My parents say not to touch him too much because his skin may be poisonous. Is this really true?

Claudia Dupont
Edmonton, Alberta

It is true that some frogs and salamanders have some stuff in their skins that is poisonous—at least poisonous enough to make a dog sick if it ate one. I am sure you are not planning to eat your newt and I doubt that there is any danger in touching it.

However, you should also think about your newt and how it will be happiest. It needs to keep its skin moist and probably does not like to be touched. It probably would like it best just to crawl under some damp leaves in your garden.

I am very interested in chameleons. I would like to know how chameleons change their color, and also when they shed their skin.

Dwayne Walker
Newport News, Virginia

A chameleon is a special kind of lizard. It has big eyes and a long tongue with which it catches insects to eat. It also has a tail that can hold on to branches, and it has a body of different shape than other lizards. As you know, a chameleon can change the color of its body.

There are no true chameleons in the United States. But there are some lizards that can change the color of their bodies. For this reason these lizards are called the American chameleons. They are also called anoles.

These lizards can change color from green to brown or from brown to green.

Chameleons and other lizards can change colors because of some color cells they have in their skins. The color is changed because these color cells change size and shape.

We do not know everything that causes lizards to change color. One thing that helps is what the lizard sees. Other things are how the lizard feels and whether it is hot or cold. Neither chameleons nor any other lizards are always the same color as the stuff they are sitting on.

The American chameleon feeds on insects. As it grows, it sheds its skin from time to time. If it gets lots of food it sheds its skin more often.

Anoles or American chameleons are found where there are many vines, plants, and flowers. They can find lots of insects to eat in places like this, and they sometimes climb bushes and trees.

O.P.B.

Can a skunk smell the odor it makes?

Melanie Lyons
Tompkinsville, Kentucky

I don't know the answer and I am not sure just how to find out. Out in the wild skunks do not always smell bad. They smell only because of a special fluid which they can squirt out of their back end. Unless it has a reason to be afraid, a skunk does not squirt. It just raises its tail and stamps its feet. For most animals that is enough of a warning.

It has been observed that when one skunk fights with another, neither of them do any squirting. So some people think that the special fluid does not smell so good to a skunk, either. But I do not know how to be sure that this is right.

Can porcupines shoot quills at each other?

Jack Busboom
Langley Air Force Base, Virginia

I do not believe that porcupines need to protect themselves from another porcupine very often. I have never seen two porcupines fighting, nor have I read that such fights occur.

Porcupines may sometimes fight during the mating season, but I do not believe such fights are especially serious. If they do fight, I suspect they swing their tails back and forth as though they were fighting some other animal. The quills that cover most of the body would protect the animals from the quills of the other porcupine. But the animals do occasionally get quills in unprotected parts of the body such as the front legs.

When a porcupine gets quilled, it pulls the quill out. They have been seen to use their front legs to remove quills that are not very deep, and to use their teeth to dislodge quills that are stuck in more deeply.

Porcupines do not pick fights with other animals. They seem to be satisfied to go waddling and grunting along, eating bark and other plant parts, and not paying any attention to what other animals are doing. They do not appear to be afraid of other animals, but act as though they are well protected. And of course the quills do give them very good protection.

Porcupines are sometimes attacked by other animals that are trying to collect a nice fat porcupine to eat. A porcupine that is attacked will erect its quills, then back toward the other animal swinging its tail back and forth. If the animal attacking is foolish enough to be hit by the tail, it often gets a face full of quills for its trouble.

O.P.B.

61

Every dog I know goes around and around in circles before lying down. Could you tell me why they do this?

Rhonda Willoughby
High River, Alberta

I have heard the idea that the circling before lying down is a behavior inherited from wild ancestors. Maybe it was a way of making a nest in tall weeds or grass.

That sounds reasonable though I cannot be sure it is the best explanation. If you find a better explanation, please let me know.

Is it true that cats, dogs, and maybe other animals can hear things that people can't?

Alisha Olmsted
Lake Ann, Michigan

Dogs can hear sounds of higher frequency, or higher pitch, than your ear can hear. You can buy dog whistles that make high-pitched sounds just for calling a dog. Recent studies on elephants show that they seem to communicate through sounds that have a pitch so low—even lower than that of a big drum—that people can't hear it.

So, I guess the answer to your question is yes.

My dog sometimes eats our grass and then throws up. Why does she eat the grass if she will throw up?

Dana Kern
Los Gatos, California

That seems a rather common thing for dogs to do. We had a dog that used to do that. I think our dog felt sick before she ate grass. Dogs throw up rather easily, much more readily than people do. It occurs to me that maybe eating grass is a way a dog uses to help it throw up.

You can see that I really do not know the answer. If I were you I would ask your veterinarian, who probably will have a simple answer.

Do dogs have good eyesight? My dog sometimes barks at our garbage cans.

Timmy Green
Chicago, Illinois

I always supposed that dogs have good eyesight. However, maybe some of them have problems with their eyes just as humans do.

I also should tell you that I have seen dogs bark at very strange things for no reason that I could understand.

Maybe you can invent some way to test your dog's eyesight. Will it run to get a stick or ball that you throw? If it can do that its eyesight must be OK. Or maybe you can think of some other trick.

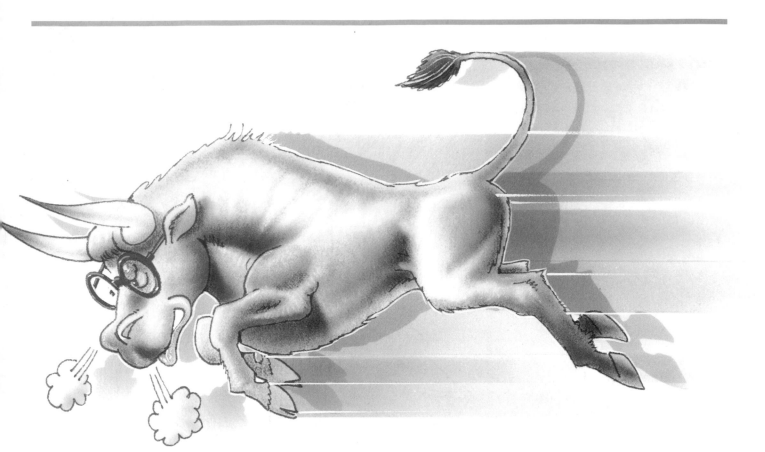

Can bulls really see red?

Sarah Arbuckle
New Boston, Missouri

I thought I knew the answer because other readers had asked me that question. The standard answer has been that, of all the mammals, only humans and apes have color vision. If that is true, then we would have to say that bulls do not see red because they are color-blind. But this idea comes from a book that was published in 1942. When I went to the library to check again, I found that there have been a lot more studies on color vision in animals since then.

Finding out about color vision in people is easy because people can tell us what they see. But how do you find out in animals?

One way is to teach the animal to play a game to see whether it can tell if two spots of light are the same or different. Can the animal tell that a yellow spot and an orange spot are different? Can it tell a yellow spot from spots with shades of gray? Not all studies have agreed.

I found one study on color vision in cows done by scientists in Poland. They found that their cows could see the differences between seven different colors ranging from blue to red. They believed, but did not prove, that a red color made cows more excitable.

I think we can suppose that bulls are like cows in their color vision. It seems that bulls can see red all right. And it might even turn out that the red color chosen for a bullfighter's cape may be the best color to excite a bull.

I also learned about a recent, very careful study of color vision in dogs. Dogs easily see differences between blues and greens and yellows. But they are not very good at seeing differences between yellows and oranges and reds. So it seems that dogs see colors about the same as some people who are said to be red-green color-blind.

I suspect that the question of whether an animal has color vision will someday be answered, not by yes or no, but by how much.

I've always wanted to know if animals such as dogs and cats have languages of their own. Do they?

Shannon Williams
Bethesda, Maryland

If you have a dog of your own or have watched two dogs playing together, you already know part of the answer. A dog has a way of telling things to other dogs, maybe just by the way it barks or growls or maybe just by the way it holds its tail.

Different kinds of animals have different ways of telling things to each other. In fact, whole books are written about animal communication. In general, it seems the social animals—the kinds that live together in groups—develop better ways of talking to each other. Most cats are loners and less social than dogs. But even a cat has a way of telling another cat it doesn't like him—at least if it wants to.

Of course, there is also another part to the answer. The things that animals can say to each other are really pretty simple. No animal could say, "I can't come out until five o'clock because I have to take care of my baby sister and then do my homework." But you might say that. You can put sounds together to make words. You can put words together to make ideas. And you do all that so well that another person knows exactly what you are thinking.

Maybe that's what you mean by "language." If you do, then you have to say that other animals do not have a real language, only ways of giving some signals for simple ideas.

I guess the answer to your question depends on what you think language really is.

Can animals catch cold or get a fever?

Brian Kirk
Newport, Rhode Island

I think the answer to your question is yes. Animals do get a fever when they are sick. I am not sure whether any other animal gets the disease we call a cold. But I suppose that every animal has its own set of diseases.

There are some diseases of animals which humans can get, too. One of these is rabies, which occurs in dogs and wild animals such as foxes, bats, and squirrels. A person bitten by a sick animal can get the rabies virus which causes the disease. Dogs usually are vaccinated to protect them from rabies.

There is one way in which diseases are less of a problem for wild animals than for people. People often live close together. And often we spend some time rather close to other people, as in buses, classrooms, and theaters. That makes it easier for diseases to be transferred from one person to another. Wild animals seldom crowd together the way we do and their diseases do not spread so easily.

Did unicorns really exist?

Tammy Tovar
San Francisco, California

I am sorry to tell you that the answer is no. The unicorn is an imaginary animal, maybe based on the stories of someone who had seen a rhinoceros. A lot of people must have liked that idea because there seem to be lots of pictures of unicorns. But no one has found any bones or fossil of an animal that could have looked like the pictures.

Why do tigers like to swim when other members of the cat family do not?

Levi Klau
Ashville, New York

I have read that tigers not only swim but even like to bathe. However, I have never seen a tiger do that.

I don't know how to answer the "why" part and I am not sure that anyone can. Most tigers live in Southeast Asia where there are lots of streams and rivers. Maybe they learned to swim just because there is so much water where they live. Lions and mountain lions live in drier country and might not have to cross streams. Do you think this is a sensible idea?

Why do certain animals live in specific places?

Shaylee Nevez
Portola, California

Each kind of animal lives in a particular kind of place, which you can call its habitat. There is a basic reason for that. In nature, animals are always in competition. They struggle to survive.

You will notice that the animals in any particular habitat seem well suited or adapted to live there. A sea lion's front and back legs have become flippers and are good for swimming. Sea lions are great at living in the ocean and catching fish to eat. You can easily see that a buffalo could never live in the sea lion's habitat. But it's also easy to see that a sea lion could never live on the grassland of the buffalo's habitat.

I guess we could say that to compete in its habitat, an animal must become a specialist. But being a specialist helps in only one habitat and is likely to be a problem in others.

Plants are also limited to particular habitats. The cactus is good at living in the desert, a water lily can live only in water, and a pine tree is good at living on snowy mountainsides.

Why is bird watching popular?

Vivek Vinair
Falls Church, Virginia

I have friends who are bird watchers. But I don't know any who say they are reptile watchers or mammal watchers or fish watchers. I guess that's why you asked the question.

Bird watching is something anyone can do. Birds move around so much that anyone can get to see them. And we can bring them in closer with feeders or birdhouses. Watching them doesn't cost much and is easy to do.

An enthusiastic bird watcher could probably give you more reasons, but perhaps you can think of some others yourself.

Do cats have souls?

Briana Bathrick
Wales, Massachusetts

That's a very heavy question and one that I am not really qualified to answer. My own idea is that you have something deep inside that is the spiritual part of you. But after I have said that I don't know what to say next.

But you asked about cats. I don't know about that or even how to find out. I did wonder why you asked the question.

Maybe you had a cat that died and you miss it very much.

Until a few years ago I had a cat, Jackie, that had lived with us for a long time. She was a people-loving cat. When my wife and I played badminton in the afternoon, she would stretch out on a bench just to watch us. I still remember all the little things she did that made us love her. Now that she is gone I sometimes catch myself looking to see if she is stretched out on that bench again.

Maybe that great memory I have could be called a part of Jackie's soul. I guess that's the best I can do in answering your question.

Could a bird on its way to the Arctic possibly get lost where I live in Bear, Delaware?

Jana O'Grady
Bear, Delaware

I just have to say I don't know. You must have seen some strange and unusual bird. I think you might look in the Peterson bird guide. It shows migration routes for different birds. Maybe you are on a flyway path for some birds.

I have wondered what could happen to one of the birds in a long nonstop flight. What would happen if one got tired? Maybe it would just stop to rest awhile. What do you think?

69

Why are bugs attracted to light? I turned on the light outside our house, and all the bugs flew around it.

Heidi Greger
Rockford, Michigan

I am sorry that I cannot tell you why bugs are attracted to light. But I can tell you a few other things about insects and light. Some bugs or insects are attracted to light, but others go away from light. We say that those that move away from light are repelled. Cockroaches are insects that are repelled by light. They usually hide in dark places such as under the sink, behind drawers, and in cracks.

Certain kinds of light attract insects more than others. White light and blue light attract them more than do red or yellow light. Some people use yellow bulbs outside their houses. Insects do not fly around yellow bulbs as much as they do around white bulbs.

Sometimes young insects are not attracted to lights, but grown insects of the same kind are attracted. For example, cricket eggs hatch in the spring. The young crickets grow in the spring and early summer. You do not see many young crickets around lights. When the crickets get grown in the late summer and fall, they sometimes get together in large groups. In some cities in the United States these grown crickets are attracted to lights in the late summer and fall.

If large numbers of crickets are attracted to lights, they can cause trouble. They fly and hop around the lights and get on people when they pass, and people do not like to be covered by flying, hopping crickets!

70

I would like to know if an insect has ears. This question has been bugging me for a long time.

Meg Wallace
Middletown, Pennsylvania

Many insects do indeed have ears, although they do not look very much like ours. And the ears of many insects are not on their heads. They are on parts of the body that seem strange to us.

The ears of grasshoppers, crickets, and katydids are rather easy to find. Those of grasshoppers are at the base of the tail, one on each side, near the last pair of legs. Each ear looks like a small, shiny piece of cellophane.

The ears are really small membranes that work something like our eardrums.

The ears of crickets and katydids are on the front legs. Each is in a very small depression on the upper part of the leg joint just above the foot. These ears also have small shiny membranes, but they are so small that the membranes are hard to see. The ears of certain other insects are on other parts of the body.

The "feelers" or antennas on the heads of mosquitoes are used for their ears. When a mosquito flies, the wings move so fast that they make a humming or singing sound. We call this sound the song of the mosquito.

The male (or papa) mosquito can "hear" or receive the female mosquito's song with his antennas. The song tells a male mosquito that nearby there is a female mosquito that is the same kind of mosquito that he is. The male mosquito can follow the song.

Why do animals have four legs?

Stacy Mackingu
Torrance, California

I guess you are thinking about the larger animals. The amphibians (like frogs), reptiles (like lizards), birds, and mammals are all called tetrapods, which means four-footed. Of course the birds have two wings instead of two legs. And humans have two arms in place of two legs. And there are some special kinds like snakes which seem to have lost their legs.

But why is four legs the general plan? I don't know.

You should also consider that the most successful group of animals is the insects. They have more different kinds (probably more than a million species), and they live in more different kinds of places than any other group. They have six legs. So maybe four is not so wonderful.

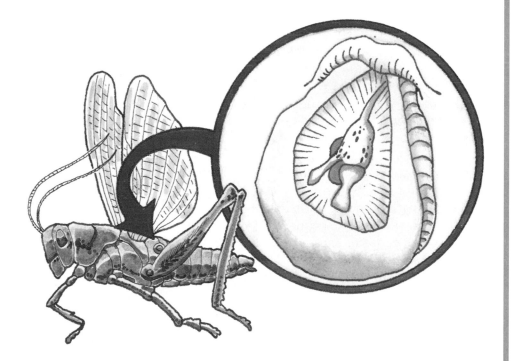

71

Why does a snake's tongue flash out?

Ronald Durbin
Rochester, New York

Almost everyone knows that as a snake crawls along, its tongue flicks in and out of its mouth. Most people also know that the tongue is forked. Both the flicking habit and the fact that the tongue is forked are unusual among animals. Because these things are unusual, some people believe that snakes bite with their tongues.

Snakes of course do not bite with their tongues, but it is quite useful to the snake to flick the tongue in and out of its mouth. The tongue is a very important sense organ. The snake, of course, has no fingers or toes with which to feel. The tongue has a sense of touch, and because of this, the tongue somewhat takes the place of fingers and toes. The snake can smell with its nose, but the tongue helps the nose because it also has a sense of smell.

The sense of touch and the sense of smell in the tongue help the snake to find its food. The tongue also helps the snake to find another snake during the mating season.

O.P.B.

In pond water there are tiny animals such as protozoans. When the water evaporates, do these tiny animals evaporate, too?

Denise Vitola
West Atlantic City, New Jersey

When a pond dries up, most of the little animals dry up and die. A few of them are covered up in the mud and leaves at the bottom and, if the pond does not get too dry, they can go on living. Some of them form cysts, which are little round bodies with tough walls which are very resistant. When they get wet again the cysts change back into normal cells that swim away.

All micro-organisms, including the protozoa, can be carried by wind or on blowing leaves or on the feet of water birds. So a dried-up pond, or even a brand-new pond, suddenly filled with water soon gets micro-organisms from outside. And micro-organisms can multiply so fast that a few starters can soon grow into thousands more.

As you can see, the life of any one individual among the littlest animals is rather precarious. Usually there are so many that we do not pay much attention to what happens to any one of them.

I heard that camels store fat, not water, in their humps. So how does fat help them survive in the desert?

Chani Lefkowitz
Brooklyn, New York

Camels do store some fat in their humps, but that is not an explanation of their survival in the desert. They let their body temperature slowly increase during a hot day and then cool back down at night. They don't sweat so much during the day, partly protected from the sun by tight hairs on their backs.

Camels don't have any one special secret. Their bodies just do several things a little differently.

Which came first, the chicken or the egg?

Anna Wilson
Liverpool, New York

I'm glad you asked. It's fun to ask a question that really can't be answered.

Suppose you start by thinking of a fertile chicken egg that hatches. The new chick grows into a big chick, and then a chicken. Then that chicken lays an egg.

You could show what happened by drawing a line:

egg—chick—big chick—chicken—egg

If you think about it some more, you'll see that a line doesn't help too much because it has an egg at the beginning and an egg at the end. And even if you started with a chicken, you'd still end with a chicken.

You could also show what happened by drawing a circle:

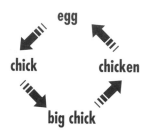

So no matter where you start, that's where you'll finish. A circle is a special kind of line, because you can start it and end it anyplace you choose.

A biologist thinks about things as a circle, or cycle. Any living organism goes through a life cycle—a process that can be drawn as a circle. The circle shows that life repeats itself over and over.

Your question doesn't have a definite answer, but we can learn something by talking about it.

Do animals cry the way people do?

Ashley Katen
Glenrock, Wyoming

Cats and dogs and most other animals have lacrimal glands. These glands produce tears, which moisten the front of the eye and help keep it clean. If some dirt gets in the eyes, the glands make extra tears that spill over and run down outside. I guess you could call that crying.

But you probably are thinking of crying as something people do when they are hurt or very sad. I have never seen any other animal do that.

The lacrimal glands are controlled by nerve messages from the brain. In your brain, you must also have some special nerve pathways that allow emotions to affect the glands. As far as I can find out, other animals do not have those pathways.

If you can find more information about this, please let me know.

I have always wanted to know what the biggest dinosaur was. Some of my books say it was Brontosaurus, some Brachiosaurus, others Ultrasaurus, some Seismosaurus, and one says it was Breviparopus.

Nicholas Goffee
New Concord, Ohio

I didn't know the answer so I asked my friend, Wann Langston, who has spent his life studying dinosaurs. Here is what he said:

There are a number of candidates that seem to be bigger than Brontosaurus. One is Ultrasaurus, another (maybe bigger) is Supersaurus, and still another (maybe bigger yet) is Seismosaurus.

Here's the problem. No one has found a complete skeleton of any of these very large, plant-eating dinosaurs. Instead we may have a legbone from one, a shoulder from another, maybe some of the backbones of another. It's easy to tell that they had to be very big animals. It's hard to tell which was the biggest.

How come dinosaurs had such small brains? To control their bodies would seem to need a larger brain.

Greg Lanier
San Jose, California

I can see why you might wonder why animals as large as dinosaurs should have small brains.

Of course, no one has seen a dinosaur brain. We know that they must have been small because of the small size of their skulls.

The dinosaur you probably are thinking about was Brontosaurus, the Thunder Lizard. From fossil bones it has been estimated that this critter weighed as much as thirty-five tons but had a brain which could hardly have weighed as much as a pound. Sometimes it is said that Brontosaurus also had a second brain at the base of its tail. Actually this so-called second brain must have been just an enlarged part of its spinal cord.

In the nervous system the job of controlling muscles and body parts is done mostly in the spinal cord. So just managing a big body does not necessarily require a big brain. The brain is the part of the nervous system which does the job we call thinking.

I suspect that Brontosaurus did not do much thinking. In fact, some people have suggested that that is one reason why Brontosaurus and the other dinosaurs perished from the earth. I guess the idea is that smarter animals came along.

How do lungless animals breathe? I am thinking particularly about insects like ants.

Jonathan Kibler
Claremont, California

Insects like the ant have a simple breathing system made of small tubes called trachea that extend from the body surface to someplace inside. Insects don't breathe the way you do, but movements of their muscles squeeze the trachea and push a little air in and out.

I know most animals have bones. But what about ants?

Tessa Butzke
Los Angeles, California

The answer is no, ants don't have bones. As other insects, an ant wears its skeleton on the outside, so it is called an exoskeleton. And it really isn't made of bone but of a stuff called chitin.

Since there are more kinds of insects than of any other group of animals, I guess we have to decide that most animals do not have bones. That may seem a surprise just because most of the big animals we see do have bones like ours.

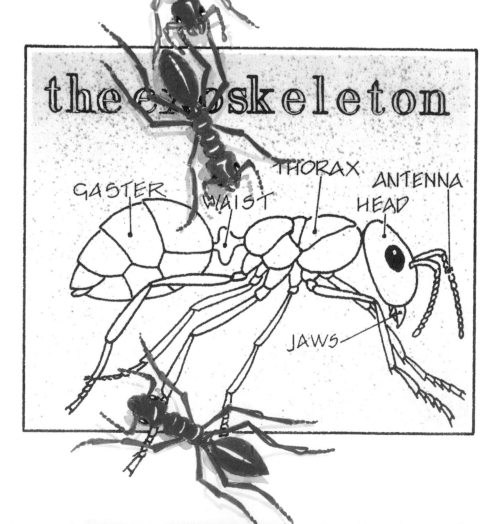

the exoskeleton

GASTER WAIST THORAX ANTENNA HEAD JAWS

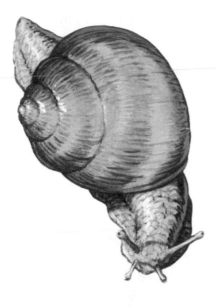

What do snails eat? And what happens when a snail does not have a shell? Does it grow a new one or find one?

Nejla Milanana
Williamsport, Maryland

There are many different kinds of snails. Most of them live on plant material. The ones that live in water usually move slowly over rocks, picking up algae as they go. Some people like to have snails in aquaria because they work like small vacuum cleaners to suck the green scum of algae off the glass.

The snails have close relatives, the slugs, which are like naked snails without any shells. The snails are their own house builders and each one makes its own shell. That seems like a lot of work. But if you watch a snail, you soon realize that it is never in a hurry and has lots of time.

Do ostriches still swallow pebbles after eating? I read about it in Swiss Family Robinson, so I was wondering.

Jodie Mangawang
Waco, Texas

I don't know when an ostrich is likely to swallow pebbles, but I would expect it to do so rather often. Like other birds, it really doesn't chew its food the way we do. Instead it has a gizzard, a pouch with heavy muscle walls, which grinds up its food.

Most birds have some grit or fine stones in the gizzard to help. So I suppose a bird as big as an ostrich would be using pebbles.

Why do a dog's legs thump when you scratch its back or tummy?

Sara Stallard
Campbell, California

I have noticed that, too. If you try that some more on your dog, you will find that you have to scratch at a special place. Scratching behind a dog's ears won't work.

I think that you are talking about what is called the "scratch reflex." This is one of those automatic actions of an animal's body. These reflexes depend on muscles and nerves but do not depend upon thinking in the brain.

The scratch reflex is complicated because it makes a lot of leg muscles work just by lightly scratching special places, usually on a dog's side. I think it is supposed to work on other animals, too.

Why aren't cats fierce and dangerous like lions, tigers, and mountain lions?

Patricia Hays
Frankston, Texas

You are right about that. Our common house cats are safe to live with. Of course, they have been living with people for several thousand years. They have become different from wild cats in much the same way that dogs are different from wolves.

You may notice that even house cats still have some wild streaks. I think we feed our cat pretty well. But she still goes out hunting for birds and mice. She sometimes makes a mess by bringing back a dead bird and scattering feathers all over our front porch.

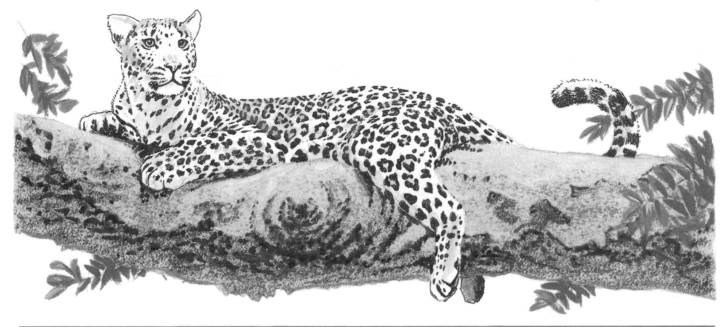

I know that the temperature of a dog is higher than a human's, but what is its exact normal temperature?

Laila Kafrawy
Flemington, New Jersey

I did not know the answer and had to look it up in a book on domestic animals. For a dog the average rectal temperature is given at 102 degrees Fahrenheit, and the normal temperature range is given as 100.2 to 103.8 degrees F. The normal rectal temperature of a human is supposed to be 98.6 degrees F.

You are right that dogs run a little warmer than humans. However, there is no exact "normal" temperature. Body temperature is not exactly the same in all individuals. And your temperature may vary about one degree during the course of a day. Probably a dog's temperature will, too.

When I looked this up I was surprised at the number of animals that have had their temperatures taken. One that caught my eye was the skunk, body temperature 97.5 degrees F. It must have taken a very curious person to find that out!

Where do fish go in the winter for shelter?

Mary Houghton
Albany, New York

I think you asked that question because in New York State, where you live, most streams and lakes are covered with ice in the winter. However, very few lakes and large streams freeze all the way to the bottom. Ice provides pretty good insulation against heat flow. And since the ice always floats as a layer on top, the water underneath is protected and doesn't freeze.

You also might think about how neat it is that ice does float. If it did not, then lakes would freeze from the bottom up, and that would be bad for the fish.

How do fish breathe?

Lora Toney
Gastonia, North Carolina

You and I usually think about breathing as the moving of air into and out of our lungs. The important event occurs in our lungs. That is where we take up oxygen and get rid of carbon dioxide.

Some water animals, such as turtles and whales, do their breathing about the same way we do. But fish and other water animals do their breathing (if we can call it that) right from the water itself. Instead of lungs, they have gills.

In most fishes the gills are just behind the mouth, one on each side. Most fishes, when they are not swimming, slowly move their gill flaps to pump water through them. If you look closely at the gills of a fish, you will see that inside they have thin, flimsy rows of red tissue. They are red because of the many blood vessels close to the surface of the tissue. That is where a fish gets its oxygen from the water.

I have four fishes in a plastic aquarium. I have noticed that the water starts to go green about four days after I clean it. Would you please explain why the aquarium goes green?

Susanna Morey
Nagano Ken, Japan

I think your aquarium gets green because of algae that grow in its water. There are many different kinds of these which are microscopic in size and made out of single cells, the tiniest of plants. When there are enough of them in an aquarium, they will make the water look greenish.

In aquariums and swimming pools, algae are considered a nuisance. In ponds and rivers and oceans algae are important because they are the plants which support all the animals that live in the water.

Sometimes algae are called the "grasses of the ocean" or the beginning of the "food chain." Here is the idea. The tiny algae are food for tiny animals; the tiny animals are food for little fish; and little fish are food for bigger fish. The best fishing places in the ocean are those which also have the most algae.

I suppose you would like to keep algae from growing in your aquarium and making the water green. Of course, there are chemicals which kill algae but most of these are not good for our fish. Algae need light and you could keep them from growing by keeping your aquarium in the dark—but that would not be much fun. However, you might try keeping your aquarium someplace which does not get too much light. And when you clean your aquarium, you should clean it carefully to get rid of all the algae you can.

You might be interested to know that I purposely grow algae in my laboratory. I have spent most of my life studying photosynthesis, the process that all plants use to make their own food using light energy. Photosynthesis in algae works just about the same as it does in the leaf of a tree. And in some ways algae are easier to manage.

I could say a lot more about algae, but maybe I already have told you more than you wanted to know.

How does an animal get its name?

Howard Cheung
Vancouver, British Columbia

Scientists who keep track of animals (and plants) have very strict rules for scientific names. The scientist who first describes an animal has the privilege of giving it a scientific name. As you may know, the scientific name is in Latin and always in two words. *Ursus horribilis* is the grizzly bear and *Ursus Americanus* is the black bear. They both belong to the genus Ursus, but each has its own species name.

Common names are likely to be different in different languages. I doubt that it is known just who invented the common names.

In school I read that reptiles lay eggs. I've been wondering if birds are reptiles or mammals.

Dawn McKnight
Gibraltar, Michigan

Birds do not fit in either classification. The animal kingdom is broken down into invertebrates (animals without backbones) and vertebrates (animals with backbones). There are several classes under the heading vertebrate including bony fishes, amphibians, reptiles, mammals, and birds.

Birds are special enough that scientists have decided to put them in a class of their own.

Are there any animals on earth that man does not know about?

Jim Gardner
Capac, Michigan

If you mean large land animals, like wolves or giraffes or elephants, then I doubt that there are any that some person has not seen. We humans are so curious that we have rather carefully explored the surface of our earth. One place we have not explored very well is the depths of the oceans.

It was a big surprise about fifty years ago when a previously unknown fish was caught off the coast of South Africa. And it was not just a little fish. It was about five feet long and weighed 127 pounds. It belonged to an interesting group of fishes called the Coelacanths. Similar fish had been known only from fossil remains which were at least sixty million years old. So this discovery was quite a surprise.

I expect that we will find new and interesting fish and other marine animals as we keep exploring the oceans.

Even on the earth's surface there are many new kinds or species of small animals reported every year. This is especially true for the insects. No one has counted carefully all the known species of insects, but a common estimate is about 800,000. Some zoologists guess that actually there may be more than one million. If that guess is right, then it means that there are a lot of insects which we do not know about—at least scientifically.

When ice freezes, how do dolphins breathe? I know they're mammals but they are in the water. They also need to breathe, though.

Melissa Stewart
Vincennes, Indiana

You asked that question because you know that dolphins are mammals. They can't get oxygen from water the way fish do. So, they have to come to the surface often to breathe air.

The answer is that dolphins don't live where the ocean freezes over, as it does close to the North and South poles. They live in the warmer oceans that never freeze over.

Do fish talk to each other underwater?

Tara Gruber
Mickelton, New Jersey

We usually think that fish are quiet, but underwater listening devices show that the ocean is a noisy place. Still, we know more about how fish listen than how they talk.

Most fish have a lateral line—a line that runs along both sides of their body. The line is sensitive to pressure changes in water, and probably allows a fish to "hear" low-pitched sounds. Most fish also have ears that are sensitive to underwater sounds.

You may have seen films of hundreds of fish swimming side by side. Suddenly, all of them change direction together—but not because they're following a leader. They change because they respond to the same noise at the same time, or because they communicate with each other very quickly.

I guess you'll have to keep your ears open for more news about fish talk.

Why don't fish get crushed by the pressure in the ocean?

Trevor Manzanares
Albuquerque, New Mexico

First, think about how air pressure and water pressure work. They have the effect of squeezing an object equally in all directions. You are living right now under an air pressure of about fifteen pounds per square inch. It's squeezing you by pushing in all directions equally, but you don't ever notice because the substance in your body is pushing back with the same pressure.

A second idea is that most solids and liquids are not very compressible. In other words, they don't get smaller when under greater pressure. Something that *is* compressible is a gas. Here's a simple experiment: Let's blow up a balloon with air and take it down in the ocean. As we go deeper, the water pressure increases and the balloon gets smaller. The gas inside is being compressed. When we do the same experiment with a balloon filled with water, the balloon will not change in size as we go deeper in the ocean. The water inside is not compressible.

In the ocean a fish is squeezed equally all around by the pressure of water. But except for a little air-filled swim-bladder, a fish is made out of material that is not compressible. So the fish isn't squashed by the water pressure.

Your body isn't at home underwater the way a fish is. That's because of the air in your balloon-like lungs.

I have a pet cat named Misty. I have noticed that her nose is wet. My friend has a dog, and its nose is wet, too. I would like to know why dogs' and cats' noses are wet?

Erin Boswell
Louisville, Kentucky

I thought that it would be easy to find an answer to that question. It isn't. A book on a lot of hard-to-answer questions has been written—and with a title exactly the same as your question. The author couldn't find a very good answer, either.

Here's what I did find out. The skin covering a dog's nose is special. It has no hair follicles that make hairs and no sweat glands. So the nose is not wet by sweat. I couldn't find reference to any special glands producing fluid in the nose.

When a dog is panting, it breathes in, mostly through the nose, and breathes out, mostly through the mouth. However, in quiet breathing, much of the breathed-out air goes through the nose. That breathed-out air is warm and very humid, and there is likely to be condensation if the outside air is cooler. That may help to keep the nose wet. And you've noticed that dogs often lick their noses with their tongues. I think that if you could lick your nose that way, your nose might be wet, too.

I think that answering your question may be difficult just because there are several parts to the answer.

How do dogs wag their tails?

Candace Drewes
Scotch Plains, New Jersey

Some kinds of dogs have long tails and some have short tails, but they are all built very much alike. The inside of a dog's tail is made up of a string of bones, something like a string of big beads. Little muscles are attached to the bones. Most dogs can hold their tails up or down, or wag them from side to side, by using these little muscles.

How do cats purr?

Robert Dubel
Phoenix, Arizona

Scientists recently found an answer to that question.

By moving a small microphone over a purring cat's body, they found that the greatest vibrations are right over the larynx, or voice box. That was no surprise because a cat's meow starts in the larynx as vibrations of skinlike folds called vocal cords. A cat's vocal cords make the meow by fluttering or vibrating in the air stream when the cat breathes out.

When a cat meows, its vocal cords vibrate two hundred times a second or even faster. But from the sound of purring, we know it must be made by something that moves steadily at only twenty-five times a second. Scientists found out how that can happen.

Besides vibrating to make a meow, a cat's vocal cords can be brought together to cut off the air flow. The muscle that does that is controlled by nerve messages sent by the brain, and these messages come twenty-five times a second. So purring is caused by the cat's vocal cords chopping the air flow to give a motorboat-like sound.

How do bees make honey?

Katrina Silcox
Gallatin, Tennessee

You may have seen honeybees buzzing around flowers. If you watch them without getting too close, you will see them crawl right down into a flower. They are searching for a few drops of the sweet nectar, or sugar water, that the flower makes.

The bee will carry a load of nectar from a lot of flowers back to the hive. Then the bees will use their wings to move a little draft of air to evaporate most of the water. What's left is honey.

I saw what I think is a horsefly. My mom says it's a moth. Who's right?

Jerome Zaha
Aurora, Illinois

Here are a few good ways you can tell the difference between flies and moths.

Count their wings. Flies have two wings, and moths have four.

Look at and listen to their wings. A horsefly has almost clear, transparent wings, and it beats them so fast that it may make a buzz. Moths usually have cloudy or colored wings, and they beat their wings more slowly and quietly.

See where they land. A horsefly likes the smell of animals and may land on you. A moth is more likely to land on a flower.

How come a bee can't see you if you stand still?

Brittany Drescher
Warren, Ohio

A bee can see you, but not in the same way that your sister or friend can see you.

Every human eye has a lens that focuses light onto thousands of light-sensitive cells packed into the retina. Each cell has a nerve connection to the brain, so your eye and brain give you a sharp image of whatever you choose to look at.

A bee eye has thousands of light-sensitive cells, too—but each cell has its own lens. That means the bee sees thousands of little patches of light, making for a very blurry picture. With all those lenses, the bee is especially sensitive to movement.

If a bee sees you standing still, it may not realize what you are. But as soon as you move, you change the patches of light in the bee's eyes, and the bee notices that right away.

Why were ticks brought into the world? I've had three dig into me. But why?

Katrina Silcox
Gallatin, Tennessee

I don't know any simple way to answer just why we have ticks. But there is a general answer. Living organisms seem to have found almost all possible ways of making a living. One way is to live on some other organism. There are lots of living things that do that. They are called *parasites*. The organisms they live on are their *hosts*.

All ticks are parasites on animals. Of course, being a parasite like a tick isn't all peaches and cream. If the right animal for it doesn't come along, it simply dies. Most ticks live mainly on furry animals and don't have much of a chance to get on humans. The ticks that got into you just couldn't find a better host.

What is the smallest mammal?

Anna Shih
New Hudson, Michigan

The smallest mammal in the world is a kind of shrew. Shrews look like very small mice, except that they have more sharply pointed noses. Few people ever see a shrew because the creatures are so small and they stay in hiding much of the time. Shrews are also said to be the shortest-lived mammals on earth. Some of them grow up and become mature in about six months, then grow old and die in a year or so.

The smallest shrew lives in parts of Europe and Africa. It has a body length of about 1½ inches, and a tail of about an inch. It is called the white-toothed pigmy shrew. The smallest mammal in the United States is also a shrew. It is also called a pigmy shrew, but it is perhaps a wee bit larger than the ones that live in Europe and Africa. Our pigmy shrew lives in parts of Canada and in the eastern part of the United States. It weighs two or three grams, which is about the same weight as a dime!

Shrews have one of the biggest appetites of any mammal. They hunt food most of the time they are awake, and they eat many times a day. One kind can eat its own weight in a single meal, and two or three times its weight in a day and a night. I doubt if a pig could eat this much. Maybe we should say that people who eat too much eat like a shrew, instead of like a pig.

O.P.B.

Questions About Body and Mind

What causes a shock, and how come it makes blue sparks?

Blair Priest
Towson, Maryland

I think you are talking about static electricity which you might generate by walking over a thick carpet. Your shoes rubbing against carpet fibers give you an electric charge by picking up extra electrons from the carpet. Then when you touch something like a doorknob the extra electrons leave in a hurry and you feel a little shock.

If all this happens in a darkened room, then you also may see a little spark that goes with the shock. And I think you are right: the spark looks blue. Before your fingers actually touch the doorknob some of your charged-up electricity jumps across through the air. That makes the spark.

Air does not carry electricity very well. It is a good insulator—until you get a great enough voltage over a short distance. Then some of the molecules of air become ionized, meaning that they become electrically charged.

Every kind of atom has its own characteristic color. You have seen the red color of neon signs made by ionized atoms of neon gas inside. Air is mostly nitrogen, and I think the blue color of the spark comes from ionized nitrogen atoms.

Why do your hands get wrinkly like a prune when you take a bath, and why doesn't any other part of your body get wrinkly?

Michele Maurice
Lincolnwood, Illinois

I have noticed, too, that my hands get wrinkly when I take a bath. It also happens sometimes when I take my turn washing dishes.

This is what happens. Your outer layer of skin is a tough protein layer made by the living cells underneath. Just like other proteins, it swells up when it is soaked in water. When you think of that layer or sheet of outer skin, you can see that as it swells up and gets bigger it will make wrinkles. But do not worry. Your skin will smooth out again as it dries.

You also asked why this doesn't happen to other parts of your body. I think that is because the tough outside layer of skin is thicker on the palms of your hands. If this idea is right, then you will find that the skin on the palm wrinkles more than the skin on the back of your hand.

When you're in an airplane, why do your ears pop?

Jocelyn Coe
Houston, Texas

I think I know what you mean, although my ears just hurt instead of popping. I always carry chewing gum in a plane because chewing helps.

Inside your eardrums are air-filled chambers. The chambers are connected by little open tubes to the air space in the back of your nose. In a plane that flies high-up, the cabin is pressurized so that its air pressure is higher than the outside air but usually less than at ground level. When the plane goes up, the cabin air pressure decreases and some air slowly escapes from your inner ear through the little tubes.

For many people the problem occurs when the plane comes down and air pressure in the cabin increases. The little tubes from the nose may not let air through fast enough. Then the air pressure in your inner ear stays low and the higher pressure of the cabin air pushes in on your eardrum. That hurts.

It helps to keep the muscles of your face and mouth working to massage the little tubes and keep them open for air to go through. That's why it helps to chew gum.

Does food taste the same to animals as it does to me?

Yisrael Jaeger
Far Rockaway, New York

I like your question because it comes just from curiosity of wondering. But it's also a question I can't answer. And I doubt that anyone in the world can answer it. We just have no way to tell.

There's another question like that about animals seeing. We can do experiments to find that an animal like a dog does see colors. But even after we know that, we can't tell how the world really looks to a dog.

Where does the weight go when you lose it?

Magdalena Zbierski
New York, New York

Your body is a machine, of course a very special machine. But like other machines, it needs energy to keep it working. It gets the energy by burning the foodstuffs that you eat to make carbon dioxide and water. Your largest amount of weight loss is in the carbon dioxide you breathe out.

Your weight really doesn't change much from day to day. So the gains and losses are pretty closely balanced. Your income of food and water is balanced by your losses in urine, feces, and the carbon dioxide and water breathed out of your lungs.

One way to tell about the loss of carbon dioxide and water that you breathe out is to weigh yourself carefully when you go to bed and again when you wake up. If you have a good bathroom scale, you may be able to tell that you lose almost a pound during the night.

Why do we shiver?

Stephanie Allen
Gainesville, Virginia

Shivering is a special way the body has of trying to warm up when it gets cold. Whenever your muscles are working, they are also giving off heat. You already know this because when you are running or playing hard you get warm. Then your body sweats, and this helps cool you by evaporation of the sweat.

When your body gets cold you can help it warm up by running or some other kind of exercise. If you do not do that, your body has its own automatic or reflex way of making muscles work just under your skin. That is what we call shivering.

What causes you to breathe without thinking about it?

Jennifer Archer
Hickory, North Carolina

We are lucky that our bodies have a number of automatic controls to keep all our machinery working right. Many of these control our inside machinery and we never know about them. You can tell about some of them—like the control of the heart—by feeling your pulse.

Breathing is interesting because it can be controlled in two ways. You can decide when to breathe. You can breathe extra fast or you can even hold your breath for a short time. But when you are not thinking about it, your automatic control takes over. So you don't have to spend a lot of time worrying about when to take another breath.

The control point for your automatic control is in the base of your brain. It gets nerve messages from many places in your body. And it regulates the breathing muscles in your chest. It makes your breathing speed up during exercise and slow down when you are resting.

Our bodies are not all alike, but when we are at rest our most common breathing rate is fourteen times a minute.

To breathe, or not to breathe: that is the question.

Sometimes I have a funny feeling that someone is watching me, or I think I'm being followed. I turn out to be right almost every time. How can people "sense" that they are being watched?

Debra Burton
Delta, British Columbia

Your question got me a little curious. I guess I have felt sometimes that there was a person behind me, and I think I could agree that my experience is like yours—sometimes they are, sometimes they are not. I think when a person is behind you, you probably get a number of messages. You may hear a slight movement. You might detect a special odor like a perfume. Even though none of these might lead you to believe the person was there, you later discover it is true.

Sometimes you think someone is following you or behind you when actually no one is there. You may have misread some clues. Or it is possible that your mind is just playing little tricks on you. I'm not sure that any of this is really a scientific explanation. I hope it's of some help, though.

Why do you get a headache if you eat ice cream too fast?

Jean Ennis
Conewango Valley, New York

I have wondered about that question, too. And I have not been able to find an answer. I think there must be some cold-sensitive nerve endings (these are called receptors) in the back of your mouth. Maybe they set off a fast volley of nerve impulses carried up to your brain when they suddenly get chilled. However, I do not think this is a very complete explanation.

What causes chill bumps on your skin?

Stacy Paulson
Houston, Texas

Chill bumps—some people call them goose pimples—happen to everyone. They are little raised bumpy places on your skin that get there when your skin is cold. This is a reflex action, one of the automatic actions your body does without any thinking by your brain. In an animal with fur this helps to raise each of its hairs to fluff up its fur. Fluffed-up fur is a better insulator and helps keep the animal warm. For you it doesn't do much good. But it certainly is not anything to worry about, either.

I am sick now and I have a terrible cough. I just had my temperature taken. I wasn't coughing until the tip of the thermometer touched the back of my tongue. What made me do this, and what makes us cough?

Michael Jeske
New Britain, Pennsylvania

Coughing helps to get rid of anything that touches or tickles the larynx (the back of your throat) or the trachea (the tube going down to your lungs). If any foreign matter gets down there, it naturally is a good idea to get rid of it. That's what a cough is supposed to do.

In coughing you take in a small breath and quickly start to breathe out. There is a sudden opening of the end of the trachea and out comes a sudden blast of air. Since it is a reflex action, we cough whether we want to or not. When you have a cold, there may be a continued tickling or irritation of the larynx and coughing may be hard to stop.

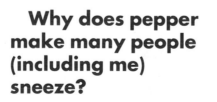

Why does pepper make many people (including me) sneeze?

Carrie Tague
El Dorado Springs, Missouri

A sneeze is a reflex action. Sometimes you can feel a sneeze coming on. But I think you cannot just decide you *want* to sneeze and then make a very good sounding sneeze.

Usually a sneeze is started by tickling or irritation of the membranes lining the inside of your nose. The sneezing reflex is useful in blowing out of your nose any dust particles causing irritation. Some substances, like pepper, contain chemicals that irritate sensitive membranes. Some of us are more sensitive than others. I guess you and I are among the more sensitive ones.

97

Everybody in my family knows how to whistle except me. How do you make the whistling sound?

Romwell Ortigoza
Kirkland, Washington

I'm not an especially good whistler, but I never thought much about what it takes to whistle. I notice that when I whistle, my tongue has to be in a special position with its tip not far back of my lips. Just making a small hole with my lips and blowing won't do it.

A whistle must be something like using a bugle or cornet or tuba or flute. These are all wind instruments. They make sound from a small vibration that makes the whole air column vibrate. That's what you try to do in whistling, set up a vibration at your lips that makes the air in your nose and mouth and throat vibrate.

After I've said all that, I know I haven't taught you to whistle and I doubt that I can. All I can suggest is that you try various positions of your tongue.

I asked my wife about whistling and was amazed to discover that she can't. We have been married for more than fifty years and I never knew that. So I guess some people can get along pretty well even if they can't ever whistle.

Why is it that when you blow out of pursed lips you produce cool air, but when you blow out of wide open lips you blow hot air?

Edward Lanier
La Grange, Georgia

I know what you mean. And I suspect there is more than one reason. Your breath probably is at your body temperature when it comes out of your mouth no matter how it comes out.

When your breath comes out slowly it feels warm, but you need to put a hand up close to it. When you purse your lips the air comes out more rapidly. Then it picks up colder, outside air that goes along with it. That cooler draft of air is moving rapidly across your hand. And moving cool air seems even cooler just because it's moving and better able to take heat away from your hand.

That does not seem like a very exciting explanation, but I think that is what's happening.

What causes a person (or animal) to yawn? Does it really mean the body needs rest?

Evelyn Graff
Massapequa, New York

Our breathing is partly under automatic, or reflex, control. You can think about your breathing and decide to breathe rapidly or slowly. But most of the time you do not think about it at all and let the automatic control do the job.

The special automatic control of breathing works from a place in the base of the brain called the respiratory center. Its job is to keep checking on the carbon dioxide in your blood. When there is too much carbon dioxide in the blood, the center speeds up your breathing to help take away the carbon dioxide.

Yawning is started by that automatic control. A yawn usually happens when you are tired or bored and probably breathing slowly and not very deeply. The automatic control turns on to make you take a deep breath. That's what you call a yawn.

Sometime you may be in a place where you would be embarrassed if you were to yawn. One way to help prevent yawning is to purposely breathe more deeply. That's easier to do (and not so noticeable) if you can get up and walk around.

If you fall down and get a cut, what causes it to hurt?

Sheran Rudolph
Norwood, Massachusetts

The hurting, or pain, really comes from a lot of messages sent to your brain by nerve endings that are damaged by the cut. When a cut or bruise hurts, that seems pretty bad. But the hurting really helps protect your body. It is saying to you: "Hey, don't do that again."

My aunt Vivian got a paper cut. Why do paper cuts hurt more than other cuts?

Mary Kochan
Cuyahoga Falls, Ohio

I think by paper cut you mean cutting into yourself with the edge of a piece of paper. I have had that happen to me. I agree that it surely hurts. But I have not seen an explanation of why it should be especially hurtful.

It might be just the surprise of getting hurt by a piece of paper. It also might be that paper is so thin that when it cuts, it cuts deeply.

When your body gets scraped or has a cut or a bite, how does it go about healing itself?

Jennifer Carlock
Bath, Illinois

Healing a cut is like repairing a part of your machinery. All animals have some ability to repair damaged parts and this is so common that the repairing has a special name: regeneration.

In some of the simpler animals, regeneration is remarkable. A starfish can rebuild a new tentacle that is cut off, an earthworm can replace much of its body that is lost, a crab can rebuild a new claw when one is lost. In larger and more complicated animals, regeneration is more limited. You cannot grow a new arm or leg, but you do have some important repair ability, especially for damaged skin.

Your skin is a special and important part of your body that people seldom think about. The outer layer of skin is made from the tough pieces of cells that are no longer alive. Underneath there is a layer of cells always multiplying and making new cells that are being pushed toward the surface. When you have a cut or break in your skin, the growing skin layer pushes new cells sidewise and these slowly close up the break.

Our bones and muscles and even some of our nerve fibers can grow more to repair themselves. Our bodies cannot repair everything, but I think it is a good thing that they can do so much. I like to think of my body as a fine piece of machinery—so good that it can even make its own minor repairs.

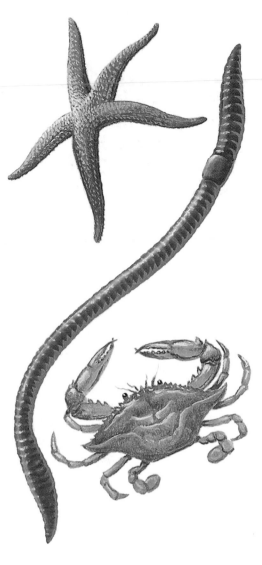

Why does your skin turn black, blue, or purple when you hurt yourself and don't bleed?

Sheryl Ordinario
Spring Valley, New York

In all the soft tissues of your body there are many tiny blood vessels, the capillaries. When you get a bruise, some of the capillaries may be broken. Then red cells of the blood leak out and collect in the tissue underneath the skin. That patch of red cells and broken-down red cells seen through the skin may look blue or even black depending on how many red cells are trapped there.

Fortunately for you, your body can repair its cuts and bruises. So the usual treatment for a bruise is to just patiently wait for the slow job of repair to take place.

I have a very bad sunburn. It is just starting to peel. I was wondering what made my sunburn peel.

Alan Houser
Monaca, Pennsylvania

As you discovered, sunburn is something painful and harmful which we ought to avoid. Those of us who have light-colored skins can easily get burned by the ultraviolet part of sunlight.

Sunburn causes real damage to the skin. Fortunately the skin is a part of our body that can regenerate by forming new cells and repairing damage. Otherwise, a wound or a burn would never heal.

Your skin is always growing slowly from new cells formed underneath the surface. Cells near the surface get squeezed down and their materials changed into a tough, horny, nonliving surface layer. That surface layer is always slowly peeling off at the outside.

When your skin is repairing itself from a sunburn, the damaged cells are pushed out faster. There is more of that non-living surface layer, and it may peel off in little patches that you can see. Then you say that your sunburn is peeling.

I went to the beach one day and got a sunburn. And I felt hotter than usual. Please explain why.

Aviva Pollack
San Diego, California

It is important to understand that a sunburn is a real burn. It occurs right in the skin surface because of damage caused by ultraviolet light. One of the results of the damage is to enlarge the tiny blood vessels just under the surface. That allows more blood to flow to the skin, making the skin look red and feel warm. It has happened to me, too, and it made me feel warm all over.

We should be more careful about getting too much sun. Getting a deep tan every summer looks healthy, but actually it is not. Ultraviolet light is likely to make your skin less flexible and more wrinkled—it makes your skin older.

I'd like to know if cracking knuckles can really cause arthritis or make your fingers fat. A lot of my friends tell me this is true. It has become a serious habit for me.

Pratima Rao
Loudenville, New York

My friend Kent L. Brown, M.D., knows much more about the answer to your question than I do, so I asked his help in answering you. Here is what Dr. Brown says:

To begin with, no one can absolutely say that if you crack your knuckles you will eventually have fat fingers or arthritis. Everyone responds differently to irritation, whether it be to a joint or a place on your skin that you constantly pick at or rub.

We do know that cracking knuckles tends to stretch the capsule, or covering that surrounds the joint, and may give you some looseness of the joint if you keep manipulating and cracking them. Also, there are medical writers who feel that mini-trauma, which means in this case a small repeated injury to the knuckle joint, could cause arthritis. These small traumas, or injuries, are repeated every time you crack your knuckles. They have what we call a cumulative effect—that is, the more you do it, the worse it gets. These little repeated injuries are different from one hard blow with a hammer or catching your finger once and bending it way back.

Cracking knuckles, then, is a form of irritation. The response of the tissue to continued irritation may cause the soft tissues (the capsule, or covering of the joint) to thicken, and this could lead to what you are calling fat fingers. It is possible that you might develop arthritis.

Cracking knuckles is a bad habit, and you should stop it. Why take a chance of deforming the joints of your hand? The hands are among the most important and useful parts of your body. They will be important when you get a job someday, just as they are now in your schoolwork and sports.

There are a couple of things you might do to break the habit of cracking your knuckles. You could carry a coin the size of a half dollar and practice manipulating it each time you have the desire to crack your knuckles. You can go to a magic store and pick up a coin-size piece of metal and instructions on how to manipulate it. I did magic for many years and found this great fun. It can occupy your whole attention.

Another thing you might do is to twiddle your thumbs. You can ask your parents or teacher how you do this. You can twiddle in one direction and then another. When you are twiddling, you won't be cracking your joints.

Hands are beautiful. You want to keep them that way. Good luck.

How come if you clap your hands underwater you can't make a sound?

Stephanie Wodejko
Bridgeport, Connecticut

I tried this and I agree with you. Clapping hands underwater doesn't make much noise, even when your head is underwater. However, if you hit two stones together underwater, you can hear their sound. Sound can travel in water, in fact about four times faster than it travels in air.

I think that clapping your hands together must make more noise than just the sound of the hands coming together. If you double up your hands to make fists and bring them together you cannot make nearly so much noise as clapping with your hands open.

So I think that clapping your hands together must compress air and make a small shock wave as they come together. I guess you could say that it is like a small explosion. Things are different underwater. Water is more viscous (less fluid) than air and you can't move your hands together so rapidly. And water is much harder to compress and make a clap. I think these are the main reasons why clapping is not so successful underwater.

Does your voice sound the same to other people as it sounds to yourself?

Annie Evans
Upper Sandusky, Ohio

I did not know the answer but I am fortunate to have a friend, Dr. Jesse Villarreal, who is a speech expert. So I can tell you what he said in reply to your question.

The answer is no. When people hear recordings of their own voices they are almost always surprised. And that is likely to happen even though others think the recordings are very good.

Here is a possible explanation. Other people hear your voice as sound waves carried in the air. You hear your own voice that way, too. But your ears also receive sound waves carried through the bones of your head. Since the sound vibrations of your voice reach your own ears by two different pathways, they probably do not arrive at exactly the same time. Anyway, the effect of the two pathways is that your voice is likely to sound a little different to you than it does to someone else.

I am glad that both of us have learned something more about our voices.

Sometimes when I go to bed it's thundering, but when I'm sleeping I don't hear it. In the morning when my mom wakes me up I hear her loud and clear. Why do I hear her better than the thunder?

Amy Wehrer
Austin, Texas

I am not at all sure of an answer, but I may be able to help you think about your question. One possibility is that you are "tuned in" to your mother's voice because you are used to it. It is also likely that your daily rhythm is set to wake up just about the time that your mother calls you every morning.

Do you think those ideas might help to explain your question?

I would like to know what an eardrum looks like and why it is called an eardrum.

Isabelle Ardila
Rockville, Maryland

The eardrum is called the eardrum because it is a tightly stretched membrane at the end of the outer opening in the ear. The membrane is like the thin and tight leather stretched across a drum.

When you tap a drum, it vibrates and makes a sound. The eardrum works in just the opposite way. Sound will make it vibrate a little. Those vibrations are picked up by a tiny bone on the inside of the eardrum, which acts as a "feeler" for the vibrations of the eardrum.

The ear is a very neat little gadget. The eardrum vibrates to a sound, but also makes a cover for the very delicate machinery inside.

In order to be able to vibrate easily, the eardrum is very thin and easily damaged. That is why it is foolish to stick anything into your ear.

Why is your mind always thinking?

Beth Dean
Kadoka, South Dakota

I like your question. I guess I never thought about why I was thinking. Really you have asked a very big question and I cannot tell you all parts of the answer. But we can talk about it a little.

Thinking is something that goes on in the brain. The brain contains millions of tiny nerve cells. Most of these have long fibers that connect them to other nerve cells so nerve messages can be sent back and forth. Some of the nerve fibers connect with longer fibers that carry messages from your eyes and ears, from tasting cells in your mouth, from smelling cells in your nose, and from touching cells in your fingers. When you are awake your brain is receiving all kinds of information by messages that your senses tell about the world around you.

So your brain always has lots to think about. Your brain can do a lot more. Suppose you think "Two plus two equals four" or "I love Mother." You are not using any of those messages from your senses. You are using something that your brain has stored up in it. Let's say that your brain can remember and can store up ideas and then put ideas together. You might say that that is how we learn.

Sometimes I think that the most remarkable part about the brain is that you can decide what you want it to think about. You can "tune in" on something almost as if you were tuning a radio to a particular station. You can tune it in to think about what you are seeing or what you are hearing, or you can tune it in on some particular idea and pay no attention to anything else.

What we have talked about really does not answer your question. But it gives you the big idea that the brain is a very busy place. As you say, it is always thinking. I think that's what the brain is for.

106

What makes people laugh?

Ayelet Yavneh
Brooklyn, New York

That's a very big question. Some things that make you laugh are physical, like tickling. No one seems to understand that very well. But most things that make us laugh are funny ideas, ideas that have an odd twist or that don't fit together, or maybe ideas said in words that have more than one meaning. Whole books have been written about what makes humor.

Of course, there is one more part of the question. Why do people laugh at something funny? I don't know the answer to that. But I'm glad they do. I think the world would be a pretty dull place without laughter. Don't you?

I would like to know how come when you tickle yourself it doesn't tickle, and when somebody else tickles you it tickles?

Joe Pettey
Vancouver, Washington

I think you have made a very interesting observation. I was not sure it was correct until I tried it on myself. Then I asked other people. Most of them think you are right.

I did notice that I feel a little tingly if I brush something very gently across the bottom of my foot. I can't do this around my ribs or under my arms, but other people can make me tickle there. I think we can agree that it is a lot harder to feel a tickle if you tickle yourself.

107

Where do our tears come from?

Lawrence Lee
San Francisco, California

Tears are always being made by little glands located above the outside corners of your eyes. They normally just ooze across your eyes at a slow and steady rate. That keeps the front surfaces of your eyes moist, and your blinking eyelids act like windshield wipers to keep them clean. The tears are carried away from the inside corners of your eyes by little tubes that lead down to the back of your nose.

Of course, most of us think of tears as big watery drops that run down our cheeks from our eyes. Suppose something hurts your eye, like a piece of dust that gets trapped under an eyelid. Then the little glands pour out tears, faster than the collecting tubes can carry them away. That's when you really know about tears, because they overflow and drip down from your eyes. You are crying. All this is brought about by a simple kind of automatic nerve control called a reflex. The reflex helps protect your eyes by washing stuff out of them.

Crying and making tears also can happen for other reasons. The reflex action is brought about by nerve messages over pathways that go through the brain. And sometimes a message can get started just by what we are thinking about. Feeling pain and feeling very sad seem to be ways that get the crying reflex started.

108

Why does crying make your nose run?

Richie Gouinlock
Alexander, New York

The first idea is that tears are being made all the time by little lacrimal glands located just above the outside corner of each eye. The tears bathe the outside surface of the eye. Then the tears are collected from the inside corner of your eyes by little tubes, the lacrimal ducts, and drained into your nose. All this is a normal and important part of the operation of your eyes.

Crying means that you are making tears extra fast—even faster than they can be drained away. That also means that the lacrimal ducts are draining tears into your nose extra fast. So your nose runs because it is filled with tears.

When you cry, the tears are salt water. How does the salt water get into your body?

Kathryn Skagerberg
Houston, Texas

Kathryn, you are very observant and you asked a sensible question.

Actually all the fluids of your body are at least a little bit salty. All of them have some salts dissolved in them and always a little of the commonest of salt, sodium chloride. (That's the one that tastes saltiest.) Your blood contains a little less than 1 percent sodium chloride and your tears probably contain almost that much. Just for comparison, seawater contains about 3 percent sodium chloride.

You are always losing some salt in your urine, so you need a continued intake of salt in your diet. Generally that's not much of a problem since there is some salt in almost all of the foods you eat. Salt is a common material in all animals and plants.

Why do onions make people cry?

Dina Rogers
Port Jefferson Station, New York

I looked up the answer in the Merck Chemical Index.

I found that onion oil contains "1-propenyl sulfenic acid, which is thought to be the lacrimator in onions." A lacrimator is something that makes your eyes water.

Now we know what the chemical is. But I am not sure that helps very much when we have to peel onions.

109

While you still have your baby teeth, where are your permanent teeth? Why do they suddenly start to pop out at a certain time?

Jenny Gower
Royal Oak, Michigan

Teeth are formed deep in the bone of your jaws. As the teeth grow and get bigger, they force themselves into position.

Your permanent teeth are already formed and growing several years before your baby teeth fall out. As your permanent teeth grow, they push out against the roots of the baby teeth. Then the roots of your baby teeth become smaller, the baby teeth begin to get loose, and finally they come out rather easily—unless you get in a hurry and pull them out.

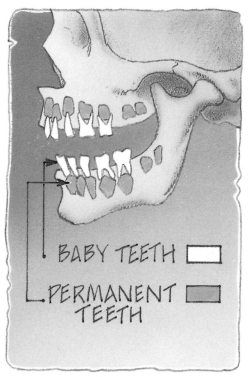

BABY TEETH ☐

PERMANENT TEETH ▨

Why do we get chapped lips?

Christine Prieto
Westbury, New York

Lips are covered by a tissue much like that inside your mouth. That's a layer that is soft and wet rather than tough and dry like your skin. Sometimes your lips may dry out and even crack open. For me that tends to happen when I get too much sun or on very dry days. I have learned that when that happens I should use something greasy to smear on my lips and protect them. Most drugstores have stuff to protect lips.

My right hand is larger than my left hand. Can you explain this?

Cathy Karnes
Hammond, Indiana

I cannot really answer your question, but I can talk about it. There are lots of reasons why one hand can be larger than the other. Sometimes this is noticeable only temporarily because something causes swelling in one and not in the other.

Many people always have noticeable differences between their right and left sides, as between their two hands. I suspect that if we made careful measurements we would find that most people have at least some small differences. Our bodies are remarkable pieces of machinery but they are not all exactly alike. And there are more differences inside than we can see outside. We know only parts of the reasons for differences.

There is a much bigger question: Why are we as much alike as we are? Why are your two hands and ears and feet as much alike as they are? Why do pigs always look like pigs, and squirrels always look like squirrels, and humans always look like humans?

Those questions are partly answered by genetics, the part of biology that has to do with inheritance. They are also partly answered by the study of development. How do animals take the information carried in one little cell, a fertilized egg, and use that information to make the whole big animal body? This is one of the most important problems of biology today. And we are a long way from answering all of its questions.

Sometimes in bed I stare at the ceiling for a while. Suddenly, the patterns on the ceiling seem to move. Why does this happen?

Micah Wilkinson
Spring Valley, Wisconsin

When you are looking at an object, the lens near the front of your eye makes an image of the object. The image falls on a thin layer, the retina, near the back of your eye. The retina contains two kinds of light-sensitive cells, the rods and the cones. They are connected by nerve pathways to your brain.

Right now in reading this, you are using the cones, which are tightly packed together at a special place on the retina. In bright light the tightly packed cones give your sharpest vision so that you can see tiny objects, even a thread or a hair.

In dim light your cones aren't sensitive enough and you can use only your rods. They are much more sensitive, but they are not tightly packed together and they do not give you a very sharp vision.

When you lie in bed in a darkened room looking at the ceiling, here's what may happen: Your eyes may be looking at a pattern on the ceiling but they don't see it very sharply. That means that your eyes may not hold steady to one spot. So the spot may seem to move just because your eyes are wandering around a little.

If this explanation is correct, then a pattern on the ceiling will not move any more if you turn the lights on. Try it and see if the pattern stands still.

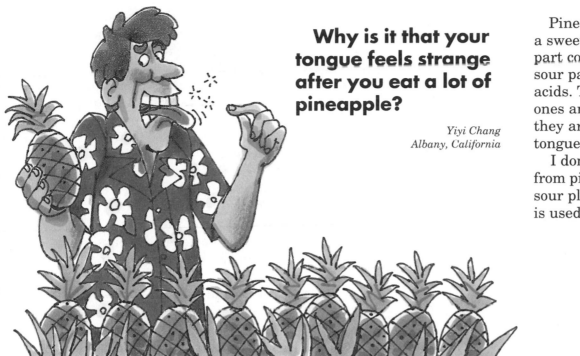

Why is it that your tongue feels strange after you eat a lot of pineapple?

Yiyi Chang
Albany, California

Pineapple is a fruit that has a sweet-sour taste. The sweet part comes from sugar. The sour part comes from plant acids. The acids are very weak ones and won't hurt you. But they are likely to leave your tongue feeling a little strange.

I don't get the effect you do from pineapple, but I do from a sour plant called rhubarb that is used a lot to make pies.

How do our taste buds work?

Andrea Essig
Granger, Indiana

I can't tell you all you might like to know, partly because not a great deal is known. The taste buds are little collections of special cells located on the surface of your tongue. Some are especially sensitive to special tastes and are grouped in particular areas: sweet at the tip, bitter in the back, sour on the sides. Areas sensitive to salt are supposed to be all over.

The sensitive cells of the taste buds are connected to a special area of the brain by nerve pathways. And different nerve messages (nerve codes) are used for different tastes. But exactly what happens to make a sensitive cell send a nerve message—much of that is still not known.

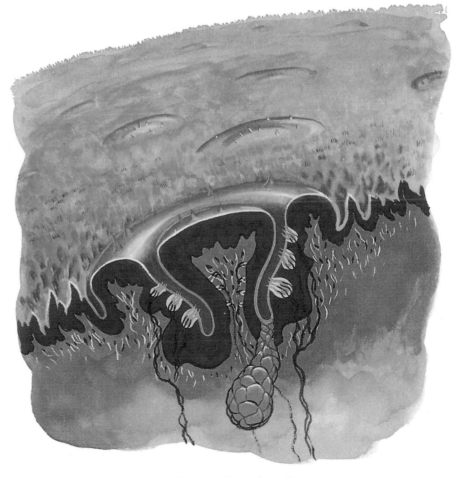

Taste buds like this one on the surface of your tongue are connected by nerves to a special part of your brain.

113

I love roller coasters, but when I ride one I don't feel good afterwards. Why do you think this happens?

Jenny Jean Myers
Woodland Hills, California

I think that the thrill of a roller coaster comes from the sudden change in forces on your body, up and down and from side to side. When you go over a hump and start down, there is an instant of time when you are almost weightless. You feel that you might go floating off in space. And at the bottom of a dip, everything in you is pressing down extra hard. Those are funny and scary feelings.

All those sudden changes in movement also make it hard for your balance control mechanism. That works in special parts of your ears to help you keep your balance. When you have long periods of back-and-forth motion—like on a rocking ship—the balance control has so much trouble that it can make you seasick. And some people get carsick to motions of a car.

I think a roller coaster gives you the thrill of sudden changes in motion but usually just not quite enough to make you sick.

Why do we throw up?

Jenny Reeves
Cranston, Rhode Island

Throwing up, or vomiting, is an automatic reflex action. It works when something irritates the lining of your stomach or small intestine. That way your body can quickly get rid of something that might be bad for you.

The reflex action of vomiting is brought about by nerve messages that go through a special control center located in the base of the brain. Naturally it is called the vomiting center. Nerve messages from other parts of the body also can reach the center and make you vomit.

One special place that sometimes gives trouble is in the inner ear. There's some special machinery there to tell you when you're right side up and to help keep your balance. That balancing machinery can get fooled by back-and-forth motion. As you probably have noticed, some people are especially sensitive. I hope you're not one of those.

What makes your stomach growl?

Lisa Turner
Heyford, England

I am not sure of the answer, but the noise probably does not come from the stomach. I think it comes from the rather violent churning that goes on all the time in the long tube below your stomach, the intestine. I suspect that the noise is more noticeable when the intestine also contains bubbles of gas produced by the many harmless bacteria that live there.

I think you will hear noises from movements of the intestines almost any time you put your ear against someone's tummy. Sometimes the noises are louder and then you may say that your stomach is growling.

I have been trying to understand snoring. My brother snores and my mother says it's from his breathing.

Kellee Boulais
Mina, South Dakota

Almost everyone may snore under some conditions, but it seems that some people are better at it than others. Snoring can be caused by a number of things that partly block the passage of air during breathing. Then the partly blocked passage of air makes the noise we call snoring.

It seems that all this is more likely to occur to a person sleeping on his or her back. And it seems to occur more often in older people.

The noise of snoring doesn't seem to bother people who snore—just other people. My wife sometimes wakes me up to stop my snoring—which had not been bothering me a bit. I also have noticed that snoring is not limited to humans. I once had a dog who snored loudly and very regularly.

You told me that your brother snores. You didn't tell me about yourself. Are you a snorer, too?

How come most people's hair turns gray when they get older?

Dana Hester
Spruce Pine, Alabama

I can tell you part, but not all, of the answer to your question. Each hair is made by a special little hair follicle that is underneath the surface of your skin. Each follicle slowly puts together the bundles of protein fibers that make up a hair. So a hair is always growing by being pushed out of the follicle that makes it. As you know, cutting off the end of a hair does not keep it from growing. So the hair you have today is not the same hair you had a few years ago.

Hair color must come from some pigment that is added by the follicle when each hair is made. I am not sure just what pigments are used to give hair its natural colors. Whatever they are, I guess that some people have hair follicles that stop making hair color when they get older. I think hair looks gray because of the lack of added color.

I have hair follicles on my head that seem to be doing a poor job. Some of them are making gray hairs. But most of them have just stopped working. There is a more common way to say that: I am bald on top.

My mom and dad are starting to have gray hairs. My mom says that if you pick a gray hair, two will grow in the same place. Is this true?

Nikki Madson
Clinton, Wisconsin

Pulling out a gray hair will probably lead a hair follicle to make another. But it won't make extra hair follicles. So I don't see how you would get two gray hairs by pulling one. However, I can understand the saying. Someone who is worried about getting gray hairs will probably keep getting more of them even if some are pulled out.

People are funny that way. When they are young, they can't wait to get grown up. And when they do get grown up, they worry about looking older. Life is more fun if you relax and enjoy it.

My hair is sensitive and it always turns light in the sun. What makes it turn?

Lori Cheshire
San Jose, California

I think you already know that hairs are made and slowly pushed out from little hair follicles in the skin. So the hair you see no longer contains any living cells. Hair color comes from pigments, such as melanin, added to the hair as it is made.

Most pigments are slowly destroyed or bleached by being out in the sun. Maybe you have noticed that colored clothes become lighter in color after being in the sun a long time. I think the same thing happens in hair.

If your hair is very black, the bleaching of some of its pigment would not be noticeable. But if your hair does not have much pigment and is already light-colored, then the bleaching of some of its pigment will be noticeable and it will become lighter in color.

Why do people have hair?

Judy Brown
Pownal, Vermont

Answering "why" is often difficult. I can tell you some things that will help you think about our hair.

Maybe the first idea is that humans belong to a class of animals called the mammals. We say that because humans and all other mammals have two features in common: mammary glands and hair. It is true that some mammals, like the rhinoceros and hippopotamus and the whales, do not have much hair—but always a little.

Hair makes a good protective covering, and many animals need it to keep warm. Most humans do not have much hair, and we have to wear clothes to keep warm. I have noticed, though, that there are rather large differences between people in how much hair they have and how it is distributed over their bodies.

Maybe you were thinking that humans do not really need hair, but I do not believe that is so. I happen to be one of those people who has lost most of the hair on top of my head. Being bald does not hurt my feelings but it certainly is no advantage. There is no cushion up there to protect me when I bump into a tree limb or a cupboard door. And on a cold day it can feel a bit chilly up there. So I believe that having hair is a good idea and I wouldn't knock it.

Why does alcohol get people drunk?

Several young persons have written to ask me this question. The answer is more complicated than you might think. I asked other people about the question and got many parts to the answer. I will try to put them all together.

Chemically, there are many different alcohols. All of them are poisons for almost all living things. One particular kind, ethyl alcohol ($CH_3 CH_2 OH$), is the least poisonous. That's the one we mean when we talk about the alcohol people drink. Only a chemist ever sees pure, 100 percent alcohol. Most of the drinks that people take have a much smaller percentage of alcohol.

After a person swallows a drink containing alcohol, the alcohol is absorbed rapidly into the bloodstream. It is then slowly removed and burned up, changing entirely in the process to carbon dioxide and water, mostly by action of the liver. The effects of alcohol on the body come from its effect on the brain. And they depend upon the amount of alcohol that builds up in the bloodstream.

As with many other poisons, a small amount of alcohol has some special effects. In small amounts it acts as a stimulant. People who are "uptight"— tense and nervous—are apt to become more relaxed and talkative, and seem to lose their worries. For this reason, some people drink a little alcohol after a hard day's work.

The trouble with alcohol begins with just a little more— just a slightly higher amount—in the bloodstream. Then it becomes a depressant. Depressants make people slower at thinking and slower at moving. But people are apt to think they are smarter and faster. That's bad. You can easily understand why they should not be driving a car.

There's another part about drinking too much alcohol that is even worse. People are likely to lose self-control. Then they are likely to drink even more. Persons who are drunk are not very nice to be around and can

be dangerous to themselves and others.

And here is a still greater problem with alcohol: Some people are compulsive drinkers. Even a small amount of alcohol "sets them off" and they keep on drinking. These people are called alcoholics. The American Medical Association says they have the disease of alcoholism.

We don't know what causes alcoholism. Some scientists think it occurs because of a small difference in the way a body's chemical machinery works.

So far no one has found a cure. The only treatment for an alcoholic is to never take a drink of alcohol—not even a little one. That may sound simple, but for an alcoholic it's not.

There is a wonderful group of men and women who call themselves Alcoholics Anonymous. They have thousands of meetings all over the country. (Alcoholics Anonymous is listed in almost every local telephone book. And information is available by mail from Box 459, New York, NY 10163.) The people who belong to Alcoholics Anonymous have found a way to help each other stop drinking and stay stopped. That's a way of treatment for alcoholism.

This is a long answer to a simple question. Alcoholic drinks have been made for thousands of years. They will always be around us. So I think everyone should understand how alcohol affects the body and that, for some people, it is part of a serious disease.

When you turn on a flashlight and put your fingers on top of the light, your fingers become bright red. Why do they do this?

Stefanie Beyer
Woodmere, New York

When a light is bright enough to go through some part of your body—like your fingers—you find out about the color of your blood. The blood going through the little tubes in your fingers contains enough oxygen that it is red.

This works best in a dark room and it works better for you than for an adult because your fingers are thinner.

What are fingernails made of?

Becky Basanda
Simpsonville, South Carolina

Fingernails are made of a special kind of protein called keratin, the same kind of stuff that a cow's hoofs and horns are made of.

There are many different kinds of proteins. You need the protein of meat or milk or plant seeds in your diet. But don't chew your fingernails. You can't digest the keratin protein.

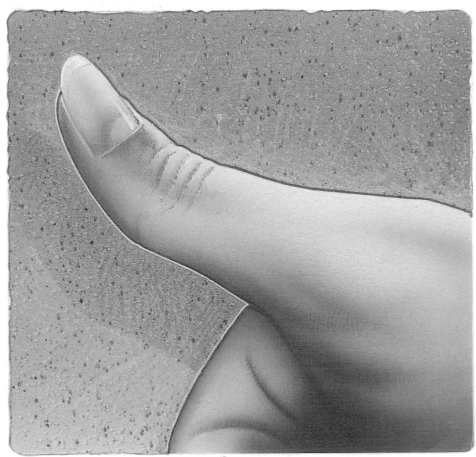

119

If you get chicken pox a first time, why are you immune to it and can't get it a second time?

Lisa Fardette
Pompano Beach, Florida

Chicken pox is a disease caused by a particular kind of virus. A virus is a very small particle, far smaller than most living cells. I think it is fair to say that a virus comes alive only when it attaches to a living cell and burrows inside. Then it mixes up the cell machinery and makes more virus particles. The chicken pox virus, once it gets into one cell of your body, multiplies to make more virus particles, which get into other cells.

Your body also has a defense against those multiplying virus particles. Most of that defense starts with some of the colorless (white) cells of your bloodstream. They recognize the virus as something foreign. They begin making protein molecules, which are inside-out copies of the virus particles—like turning a glove inside out to fit your other hand. These new protein molecules have a special name: antibodies. Each antibody protein molecule can put a virus particle out of business.

As your body makes more and more antibodies, it begins to mop up the virus particles. The effects of the chicken pox virus are not very severe and most people begin to get well in a few days.

Now you see how you get immune to chicken pox. Maybe you can guess that there is a second part of the answer to your question. You will stay immune and never get chicken pox again if your blood cells keep making antibodies against the chicken pox virus. That's what usually happens.

There are other diseases caused by other kinds of viruses. Your body works in the same way against all of them. But it does not always win so easily, and the immunity does not always last so long.

There are many other parts to the story of immunity. I have talked about a part that answers your question.

Why do we close our eyes when we sneeze?

Melissa Jones
Newberry, South Carolina

I had not noticed that but I think you are right. Some people I have watched do close their eyes during a sneeze. You are very observant.

I do not know just why that should be. A sneeze is a complicated reflex action. That means an automatic action, not one you have to think about. It is complicated in that it results from a whole series of movements. First, you take a quick breath inward, and then you breathe outward very forcefully. Usually your tongue gets in the act and partly closes off the back of your mouth so that air is forced out rapidly through your nose. The whole reflex works to get rid of something that was irritating the soft lining of your nose.

Now it seems that, at least for some of us, closing the eyes is also part of the complicated reflex. This is not a complete answer to your question, but it is the best I can do.

I would like to know what ESP is. I would like to have a few examples of it, too.

Susan Haddad
Whitewater, Wisconsin

ESP stands for Extrasensory Perception. I will try to tell you what that means.

We have many legends about people with supernatural powers. Some were supposed to be able to tell ahead of time that an event would happen in the future. Some of them were supposed to be able to tell what someone else, maybe miles away, was thinking or doing. Even today there are people who claim to have such special powers.

Every once in a while someone has a strange dream that turns out to be true. Suppose you had a dream like this. Your aunt Jane is sitting in a rocking chair with her cat on her lap. Suddenly the old chair breaks, Aunt Jane and the cat fall over backward, and she breaks her glasses. Then suppose you later discovered that what you dreamed had actually happened—even about the cat and the broken glasses and even on the very night of your dream. You certainly would be surprised. You would say to yourself that there must be some way that you could tell what was happening to Aunt Jane.

What we have been talking about might be explained if we humans sometimes had an extra sense, a sense other than seeing, hearing, touching, tasting, or smelling. That would be saying we have Extrasensory Perception.

Proving that there is such a thing as Extrasensory Perception is very difficult. It cannot be proved by human experiences like the dream we talked about.

How about all the other dreams that never come true? Even the most unlikely combinations of events sometimes happen just by chance. Proving that there is no such thing as Extrasensory Perception is also very difficult. I think that most scientists who ought to know about this, like psychologists, do not believe in it.

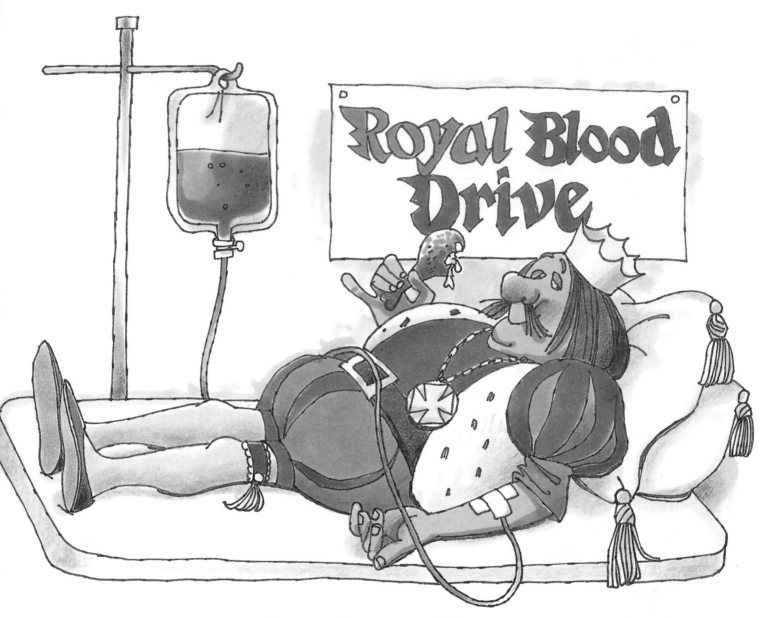

Is it true that we have blue blood?

Patsy Nightingale
Chickasha, Oklahoma

The answer is yes. But your blood is blue only in a special part of your body.

The color of blood comes from a stuff called hemoglobin. It is carried in your red blood cells. Its job is to carry oxygen from your lungs out to all the cells of your body. The color of hemoglobin depends on how much oxygen it has.

After passing through the lungs, your hemoglobin has a full load of oxygen and is red. That red blood is pumped by the heart out through your arteries. If you have a cut, it is likely to be this red arterial blood that leaks out.

From the arteries the red blood flows through very tiny tubes called capillaries, which carry it close to all of the tiny cells of your body. That's where the blood loses its oxygen. When that happens, the hemoglobin changes color and, if it loses almost all of its oxygen, it becomes dark blue. Blood from the capillaries flows into larger veins and back to the heart and lungs.

So it is only your venous blood, the blood in your veins, that may be blue.

I have heard that we have about 200,000 miles of blood vessels. If this is true, how can that many miles of blood vessels be in us?

Julio Miyares
Queens Village, New York

I am not sure of the exact number of 200,000 miles of blood vessels. No one has ever measured it. No one has even counted the number of the very tiny blood vessels, the capillaries. However, we can measure how big around they are and how much blood they must hold. If we know that, we can figure out about the length of them all put together.

Λ grown man has about six quarts of blood. At any one time most of that is in the tiniest blood vessels, the capillaries. Each capillary is less than one-tenth as big around as a human hair.

I will not bore you with all the numbers but when I figured this out I came out with about 50,000 miles of capillaries. Very likely your figure of 200,000 miles may be more nearly correct.

These numbers can be very large because the capillaries are so very small. Of course, the blood pumped by your heart does not travel all those many miles before it gets back to the heart again. Each capillary is also very short. There are many millions of those tiny, short tubes side by side all carrying blood at the same time.

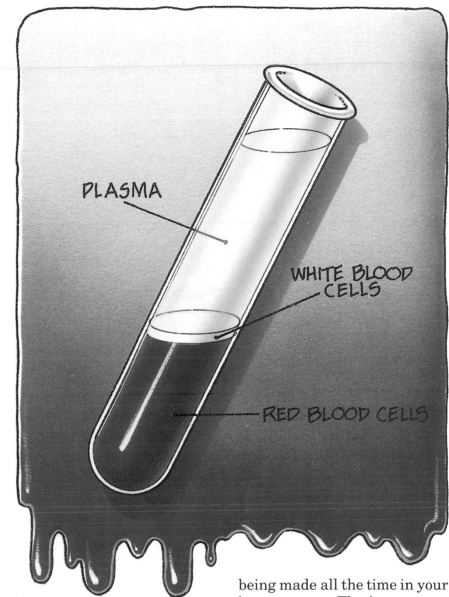

PLASMA

WHITE BLOOD CELLS

RED BLOOD CELLS

How do we get our blood?

Vaughn Lui
Honolulu, Hawaii

Blood is part of the machinery of your body and is pretty wonderful stuff. It contains a number of different things that are made in different ways.

Let's talk about the red blood cells. They make up almost half of the blood.

New red blood cells are being made all the time in your bone marrow. That's a spongy red tissue on the inside of your large bones. As they are made, the new cells are filled with hemoglobin, the stuff that makes them red and does the big job of carrying oxygen.

Your bone marrow has to keep working all the time because some red blood cells are always breaking down and need to be replaced.

Just while you were reading this, your bone marrow made several million new red blood cells. You can see that it keeps pretty busy.

A lot of people in my class don't eat breakfast. Why do we need three meals?

Mandy Byrd
Fulton, Kentucky

The standard answer has been that your body needs nourishment spaced over the day to function properly. People who have studied the problem have always said that it's important to start with a good breakfast.

There have even been some people who had the idea that kids who didn't start with a good breakfast didn't do as well in school as they would otherwise. However, there's some dispute about all that, even though I personally think it's important to start with some fuel at the beginning of the day.

There's another part to your question. Why eat only three meals a day? There have been lots of humans who didn't eat three meals a day on a regular schedule. If you think about animals in the wild, they tend to eat when food is available and not on any special schedule. And some farm animals, especially pigs, are given the choice of eating whenever they feel like it.

Eating three meals a day has become a custom. I noticed that people in the office where I work all go to lunch at noon. That is their custom, and they eat then, whether or not they are hungry. In Europe, most people tend to take their larger meal at noon and only a light supper at night. So how we divide up our meals depends a lot on custom.

I wish you would please tell why our bodies need food.

Teresa Anne Rieger
Marshfield, Massachusetts

Sometimes it helps to think of your body as a special kind of machine—a rather wonderful machine and special because it is you. Like any other machine, it needs energy to make it work. That's one reason you need food. It gives your body the energy it needs to keep working. Some foods have more energy than others. Sugars and starches and fats are useful as food because of the energy they provide.

Your body also needs food for another reason: It is always repairing itself. When you are young and growing, it is making more body machinery. Body machinery in all living things is made of protein. So you need foods like meat, eggs, and milk to provide protein. Besides the protein, your body needs a collection of spare parts called vitamins. You can get your vitamins from many foods, especially in fruits and green vegetables.

We have been learning about photosynthesis in my science class. I was wondering if a human being could live like plants, just needing water and sunshine.

Vanessa Wu
Dallas, Texas

That does sound like a great idea. But I'm afraid it would work only for science fiction. In real life it won't work. Let's think about it.

Animals and plants are built in very different ways. Animals get their food by eating. So they have to move around to find their food—and to keep from being eaten by bigger animals.

Plants make their own food by using the energy of sunlight. So they just stay in one place and don't need machinery like muscles to move around. Of course, plants have their own set of problems. One problem is that they need to catch lots of sunlight. So they make many thin, flat leaves.

For a plant to make as much food as your body uses each day, it would need a lot of leaves. Even though plant leaves are not all alike, I think it would take about 100 square yards of leaf area. That's enough leaves to cover more than 100 card tables. And you would need enough branches to hold all these leaves up to catch sunlight. Maybe you can picture yourself with an apple tree growing up over your head.

I guess you can see that animals and plants have very different problems in making a living. In order to make like a plant, you would need more than just some of that green stuff. You would need a whole new plan for your body.

I know that I dream in pictures. But how can people born blind see in their dreams? Or can they?

Brad Wixen
Los Angeles, California

I had never thought about your question and did not know an answer. So I sent your question to people who might know the answer. You will find below an answer given to us by Barbara Collins of the Braille Institute of America.

"The letter from Brad Wixen about dreams provoked quite a bit of discussion around here. The question has come up before, but no one has ever researched an answer.

"We asked our staff psychologist, who has been blind since the age of sixteen, and a blind counselor. Their answers are based on personal clinical research.

"What we dream is based upon what we experience. A sighted person dreams in pictures because that's how he experiences life. A blind person relies on his other senses, such as hearing and touch, to experience life. Therefore, he dreams by use of these other senses.

"A person who can't see cannot have a visual dream. A sighted person who has a nightmare might dream about an ugly-colored, scaly creature, created from a combination of his imagination and things he sees every day. A blind person dreaming about the same monster would hear his loud, hollow voice and feel his slimy skin. It's interesting to note that a person blind from birth doesn't realize he dreams differently from a sighted person.

"Some people who are blind have partial or residual vision. These people can see in their dreams, but only to the extent they can see in real life.

"A person who is born sighted and later loses his eyesight dreams in pictures. However, everything he sees in his dreams is based on memory. Although he knows people change (by aging, gaining weight, dyeing their hair) he never sees these changes in his dreams."

I am grateful to Barbara Collins and the Braille Institute for giving us an answer to Brad's question.

My mom and dad say I sleep talk. Why do people sleep talk?

Christy Rasp
Fallbrook, California

That's something I don't know very much about. And I suspect that no one knows a great deal about it. Scientists who study sleep and dreaming think that sleep talking is something separate from dreaming. I have read that it occurs during light sleep but not during the "rapid eye-movement" or REM sleep when most dreams occur.

I guess I can't help you very much except to say that I don't think sleep talking is anything strange or anything for you to worry about.

What is the cause of sleepwalking?

Sandra Roelcke
North Bay, Ontario

I have heard about sleepwalking, but I do not really know much about it. I will tell you some of the things I have read about it.

First, you should know that all of us move around a little even when we think we are fast asleep. Almost everyone has eye movements and many people show lip movements. Everyone has dreams. So I suppose that sleepwalking might be like acting out a dream.

Sleepwalking has a special fancy name: somnambulism. But the fact that we have a fancy word for it does not mean that we understand it. I have read that some people think that sleepwalkers are just absent-minded dreamers. So far as I can tell, there is no danger in waking up someone who is sleepwalking.

127

How come your eyeballs don't fall out when you look down?

Marc Petro
Leland, Mississippi

I guess your question arose because you were thinking of your eyes as being separate from the rest of your body. Actually, they are not.

At the back of the eye is a bundle of nerve fibers that carry messages to your brain. There are a lot more attachments made by the six muscles for each eye. These work together to turn your eyes so you can choose what you want to look at.

You can see that your eyes are pretty well anchored and not in danger of falling out.

I know people can be allergic to certain foods, dust, and animals. But can a human be allergic to water?

Rachel Glueck
Prairie Village, Kansas

I think nobody can be allergic to water. The body of every living thing needs to contain a lot of water just to be alive. Your body is about 60 percent water. If your scales say that you weigh 80 pounds, stop and think that 48 pounds of that is water.

You can see why it is hard to imagine anyone being allergic to water.

I love to go swimming, but there's too much chlorine in the water and I get red eyes. Can you tell me what to do?

Candy Bays
Newton, North Carolina

I can't solve your problem, but I can tell you why it happens. Chlorine is a very reactive chemical. It oxidizes most organic matter and will kill bacteria. It is used in our water-supply systems to kill bacteria so that the water will not carry any disease germs. Chlorine is also used in swimming pools for the same reason.

If chlorine can do all that, why isn't it dangerous to our bodies? Really it is. Actually chlorine is a poisonous gas. In water supplies and swimming pools it is used very carefully. Only very small amounts are used. And any "extra" chlorine, which does not react quickly with stuff in the water, gradually disappears. Some is lost in the air. Whatever is left is rapidly changed into harmless compounds by the action of sunlight. So the trick in managing a swimming pool is to use just enough chlorine to kill all the bacteria and not have very much left over.

A little chlorine in the water does not bother you very much partly because your body is covered by a tough skin. You have a few sensitive places not covered by skin, like the lining of your mouth and nose and your eyes. I don't like the chlorine of swimming pools, either. But I would rather have the chlorine than the diseases that would come if we did not use it.

What colors do color-blind people see?

Robin Henderson
Gainesville, Florida

I think the answer must be that they see in various shades of white to gray to black, maybe as in an old-fashioned black-and-white movie.

However, there are various degrees of color blindness. I am partly color-blind—or, really, not very sensitive—to red. When I see a traffic light a very long way off I can see a light but I can't tell whether it is red or green until I get closer.

Actually the color-sensitive cells in the retina of your eye discriminate between colors only in bright light. In very dim light your eye can't see colors as colors.

Why do we blink?

Windi Hornsby
Indianapolis, Indiana

I guess you've noticed that your eyes blink rather regularly. Most people blink about twenty-five times a minute while they are awake. Tear glands in the outside corners of your eyes are always making tears, and the blinking of your eyelids wipes them away. That keeps the front surfaces of your eyes moist and clean.

Blinking is controlled by a reflex, an automatic nerve action. Besides working regularly, the automatic control also works to close your eyelids when something is about to strike your face. So blinking is important in protecting your eyes.

You can decide not to blink and stop blinking, maybe for ten seconds or so. But then the automatic control becomes too strong. There is only one safe and effective way to stop blinking: Close your eyelids and go to sleep.

Why do people have eyebrows?

Joy Harvey
Browns Mills, New Jersey

Not much is written about eyebrows even in books about the human body. They do help add to the protection of your eyes by sticking out on the bony ridges just above. They also help to shield the eyes from glare on a bright day.

You may have noticed that some football players paint dark streaks just below their eyes. I suppose they are helping the eyebrows cut down on glare.

When I watch movies or get in trouble, I cry sometimes. When I cry, I get heavy headaches. Why is that?

Angela Marie Lawhorn
Pasadena, Maryland

I doubt that I can explain that. The best I can do is to tell you something general about headaches.

Headaches are common. I do not know anyone who could say that he or she never had a headache. Maybe one reason they are so common is that there are many possible causes.

We get aches and pains because our nervous systems have special little gadgets called pain receptors. You have a lot of these in your head, mostly outside of your skull, but not inside your brain. I think most of my headaches occur when I get tense and the muscles tighten up in my neck and scalp, or sometimes when I get a cold and my nose gets plugged up.

Sorry I can't tell you more. Your doctor could explain this better than I, and if you have many headaches it might be wise to ask him or her.

Do you know why people feel like they have a lump in their throat when they are going to cry?

Ashley Katen
Glenrock, Wyoming

I think I know what you mean, and it is a very common expression. I have never seen an explanation and I don't really know an answer, but I can think of a possible answer.

Crying occurs when the lacrimal glands of your eyes make tears faster than they can be carried away in the little tubes that drain into the back of your throat. Maybe before you really know you're crying there's an extra amount of tears going down these tubes to your throat. That would give some extra fluid in your throat and make you want to swallow. It might feel like a lump in your throat.

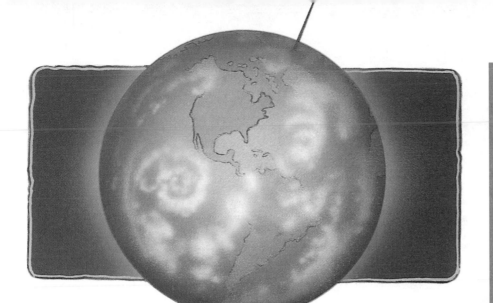

When the Earth turns around, why don't we feel it?

Corinne Etelman
Prospect Park, New Jersey

Let's see if we can find the answer by imagining that we will do this experiment together. We will get inside a moving van, with a light inside, but all closed up so that we cannot see out. Then we will ask the driver to find a long straight road and drive at a constant speed. You and I are going to sit on the floor and play checkers.

Now if the road is straight and flat and smooth, and if the driver is very careful to keep us at constant speed, you and I will not know we are moving at all. There is just no way to know. And our checkers will stay right there wherever we put them—everything around us is moving just alike. After you have won the game, as my own children usually do, we will ask the driver to make a sudden stop. We had better hang on to something. When the truck begins to stop, we will feel that we are moving. And if the stop is really sudden, those checkers will be scattered against the front of the van.

Now here you are again, reading this book. You are sitting in a chair in a house on the surface of the Earth, moving ever so fast but very smoothly as the Earth rotates and travels in its orbit around the Sun. If we couldn't see the Sun and the stars we would not know that we were moving at all.

Maybe you think my answer was not quite fair. Maybe you have heard people say that the Earth is spinning, and you are worried about its centrifugal force. It does spin, but turning around just once a day is a mighty slow spin. Put a knitting needle through the center of an orange and try to turn it that slowly, once around in a day. You will see what I mean by a slow spin. Even for the much bigger size of the Earth, the centrifugal force tending to spin us off is so much smaller than the force of gravity that we never know about it.

When you spin around a lot, how come you get dizzy?

Steven Marsh
Garland, Texas

You know that your ears do for you the important job of hearing. The inner parts of your ears also do another job: They give you a sense of balance. Deep inside your ears are some special cavities filled with fluid. Inside these cavities are sensitive little hairs attached to nerve cells. Any movement of your head makes the fluid slosh around. That bends the little hairs, and the nerve cells tell your brain about the movement.

When you spin around, there is a short time lag before the fluid spins, too. So you feel that you are spinning. When you stop, the fluid keeps spinning for a while. That may make you feel that you are spinning backward. We call that being dizzy.

133

How come it hurts when I pinch my skin, but when I pinch my hair it doesn't hurt?

Emily Ohnemus
Cooper Landing, Alaska

Your skin has many little nerve endings that warn you by pain messages when something bad happens to your skin. Your hair is made by special little hair follicles in your skin. Once a hair is pushed out of a hair follicle, it is no longer alive. And it has no nerves, so it can't feel anything when you pinch or cut it.

If hair were like skin, getting a haircut would be pretty painful.

As people get older, how come they get wrinkles?

Kim Haslam
Wethersfield, Connecticut

Skin is an important tissue that does a lot for us, like being a protective coat. The living part of your skin is an inner layer of living cells. They are continually working to make tough protein material that will become the outer layer. They also make some elastic fibers that help pull the skin tight around you.

I think that as your skin gets older, the inner layer doesn't work as well to make new stuff. And it makes fewer elastic fibers. Then the skin seems rougher and tends to wrinkle.

Sunlight is hard on your skin. Getting a tan may make you look healthy, but it helps your skin get older.

When I clap my hands, they make a different sound each time. How do they do that?

Larissa Young
Aliquippa, Pennsylvania

I had never thought about that question, so I tried clapping in different ways. You are right. My hands make different sounds depending on how I clap them. Most of the noise made by clapping comes from the air that is squeezed and compressed as your hands come together. You might think of the noise made by bursting a balloon or by breaking a blown-up paper bag. Balloons and paper bags are not themselves very noisy. Breaking them sends out a sudden pressure wave into the air. And that's what sound really is.

The palms of your hands are somewhat cup-shaped, so they are good at compressing air when they come together. That's the loudest clap you can make. The quietest clap you can make is to spread out the fingers of both hands and just let your fingers come together. You can see why they can't compress much air and make much noise.

Why do our faces turn red when we stand on our heads, but our toes don't turn red when we stand up straight?

Holly Lemon
Shiloh, Ohio

I like your question because it shows that you are a careful and curious observer.

The answer lies in the way your body manages its flow of blood to various parts of the body. It does this mostly by control of muscles in the walls of small blood vessels, called the arterioles. When these muscles tighten in one place, less blood flows through.

Your body is used to being in an upright position, so the arterioles in your feet work to limit the amount of blood down there. When you stand on your head, the control of arterioles in your face evidently is not as good. Then more blood flows into the skin of your face and makes it look redder.

What makes you blush?

Ben Hodgins
Aiken, South Carolina

What you are talking about usually happens to the skin of your face. The skin appears red because extra blood is being carried in the tiny blood vessels just under the skin.

Your control of body temperature depends partly on the control of how much blood is carried to your skin. When your body is too warm, it automatically sends more blood to your skin. That helps you lose more heat. When you are too cold, more blood is circulated deep inside and less to your skin.

Some of this control of where your blood goes works for particular parts of your skin, like your face. The control point is called a **center**, located deep in the brain. It works automatically (without thinking) but in some strange way it is affected by what you are thinking about. That's what causes a blush when extra blood is sent to the skin of your face.

What causes you to breathe without thinking about it?

Jennifer Archer
Hickory, North Carolina

We are lucky that our bodies have a number of automatic controls to keep all our machinery working right. Many of these control our inside machinery, and we never know about them. You can tell about some of them—like the control of the heart—by feeling your pulse.

Breathing is interesting because it can be controlled in two ways. You can decide when to breathe. You can breathe extra fast, or you can even hold your breath for a short time. But when you are not thinking about it, your automatic control takes over. So you don't have to spend a lot of time worrying about when to take another breath.

The control point for your automatic control is in the base of your brain. It gets messages from many places in your body. And it regulates the breathing muscles.

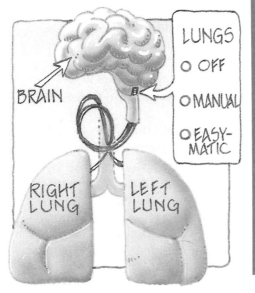

Would you please explain why we need fresh air? For instance, if you were in a box, why would you die? There is air in the box.

Monna Gaugler
Elysburg, Pennsylvania

The living machinery in the cells of your body is powered by a slow "burning" of stuff that comes from your food. So all of those cells need a supply of oxygen and are making carbon dioxide. Your blood carries oxygen from the lungs to all of those little cells and then takes back the carbon dioxide. And breathing air into and out of your lungs brings in oxygen and gets rid of carbon dioxide.

Each day your body uses up about 600 quarts of oxygen and gives off about 500 quarts of carbon dioxide. About one-fifth of the air around us is oxygen, so you could say that you take up each day all the oxygen from about 3,000 quarts of air. But you could not live all day if you were tightly sealed up in a box about the size of the inside of a small car with 3,000 quarts of air. Two bad things would happen. When you had used up about half the oxygen, the amount and concentration left in the air would be so small that your lungs and your blood could not get oxygen fast enough. But long before this happened you would be gasping because of all the extra carbon dioxide that your body had put into the closed-up volume of air.

I am glad that our planet has so much air and so much oxygen that there is plenty for all of us.

How does sweat form?

Sarah McMurray
Oxnard, California

Sweat is made by very many—maybe several million—little sweat glands scattered around in your skin. They are more tightly packed on the palms of your hands and the soles of your feet. When seen in a microscope, each gland looks like a coiled-up tube with an opening on the surface of the skin. Its job is to make sweat, which evaporates from the skin and cools your body.

The making of sweat is partly controlled from your nervous system by an automatic reflex. This normally works to make extra sweat when your body gets too warm. When the air temperature around you is above 99 degrees Fahrenheit, you need to sweat just to control your body temperature. Your body usually makes maybe a pint of sweat a day. That much evaporates so easily that you will not notice it. But that might increase to as much as five or ten quarts a day if you are very warm.

Sweat is a dilute solution filtered out of the blood. It is mostly water, with a little salt and a very small amount of organic chemicals. When first made, it is said to be odorless. Evidently, the action of bacteria on the skin causes the odors that some of us have in our sweat.

My mother used to tell me that it was more polite to say "perspiration" than to say "sweat." That may be true in parlor conversation. However, in talking about the operation of the body, sweat is the right and proper scientific word for us to use.

Does caffeine stunt your growth? My friend says he drinks coffee in the morning, but he still grows.

Kati Pederson
Valley City, North Dakota

I remember that when I was your age I heard the idea that drinking coffee would stunt your growth. I have wondered about that idea but I have never been able to find it in medical books.

The caffeine that is in tea and coffee is actually a drug, a mild stimulant. You will notice that not all people respond to it in the same way. Some people become addicted and even get headaches if they go a long time without coffee. And many people who do drink some coffee do not drink it at night because it keeps them from going to sleep.

Many adults seem to need coffee to get themselves awake in the morning. Young people don't need that. So why drink coffee? It may not do much harm but no one will argue that it is good for you.

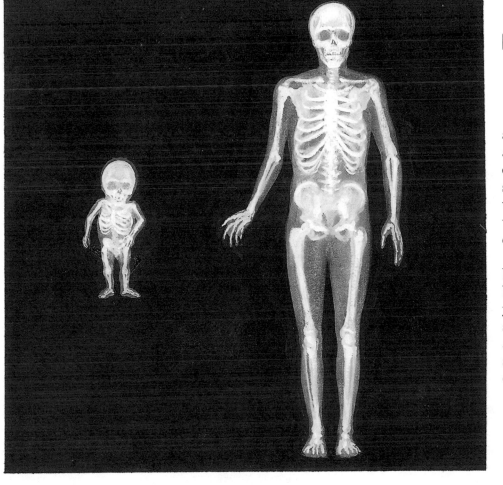

How do our bones keep getting bigger?

Christopher Hallett
Carver, Massachusetts

Bones that we see look hard and solid. In your body, bone is a living part of you. It has its own special blood supply and special cells for making or taking away the hard stuff, which is made mostly out of calcium and phosphate.

Throughout our lives our bones are slowly changing or being remodeled. At your age your bones are increasing in size and length. After middle age, bones tend to decrease in size and most people actually decrease a little in height.

What makes people float?

Amy Ripbergen
Milton, Indiana

I guess you mean float on water when you are swimming. I think the main reason is that your lungs always contain a sizable amount of air. Even if you breathe out as hard as you can, your lungs will still contain almost three pints of air. And if you take a deep breath, they will contain much more. So your body is a little like a bottle full of air.

People are not all alike in their lung capacities, and I suppose that's why some people seem to float more easily than others.

Why do people burp?

Rosabelle Lugos
San Pablo, California

When you get some gas in the stomach, three things can happen to it. The gas may pass on through to the small intestine, it may be absorbed into the blood stream through tiny blood vessels in the stomach wall, or it may come back up through your esophagus to your mouth. In order for it to come back up, a little valve must open to let the bubble of gas out of the stomach. That's when you burp.

How does gas get into the stomach? Sometimes it gets in with a little air that is swallowed. Sometimes it is dissolved in food or a drink.

You have seen soda water fizz with bubbles of carbon dioxide when you pour it into a glass. Even after you drink it, the fizzing keeps on going and makes carbon dioxide gas in the stomach. That's a good way to get a burp.

Body machinery is not exactly the same in all people. I have noticed that some people burp more than others, but I do not know why that is.

There is an interesting burping problem that I have wondered about. Some people won't eat cucumbers because they say that cucumbers make them burp. And I notice that there are now special varieties of cucumbers that are said to be "burpless." I wonder what the special chemical is in cucumbers that makes some people burp. If we know that, we might know more about the answer to your question.

Would you please tell me why we hiccup and what causes this to happen?

Donna Cameron
Lawrence, Massachusetts

First we should think about the way we normally breathe, because a hiccup is a special kind of mistake made by the breathing mechanism.

Just above your stomach and below your lungs is a sheet of muscles called the diaphragm. It completely separates the upper, or lung, cavity from the lower, or abdominal, cavity of your body. Normally this is a little dome-shaped so that it curves upward. When you breathe in, the diaphragm does most of the work by contracting and becoming flatter. And this pulls air into the lungs.

You can control your diaphragm if you want, but most of the time you do not think much about your breathing. You don't spend much time deciding when to take the next breath. You don't have to because the diaphragm is also controlled by one of those automatic reflex actions of your nervous system. The automatic action uses a special large nerve, the phrenic nerve, to carry its messages to the diaphragm.

In hiccups there is a mistake, or at least an unusual action, of the automatic control. The diaphragm is made to contract and move downward suddenly with a very strong force that sucks in air very rapidly through the windpipe down into the lungs. The automatic control often keeps repeating its error to make hiccups come rather regularly again and again. This can be mighty annoying.

Hiccups seem to be caused by irritation of the diaphragm or the phrenic nerve. Over-eating or indigestion may cause the stomach to rub against the diaphragm. Or even laughing a lot can irritate the diaphragm.

The reason that there are so many cures for hiccups is that they generally cure themselves. However, some people have had hiccups for as long as several months and have needed medical treatment to get rid of them.

Would you please explain why, when running, people often get side aches? This seems to happen mostly when people have just had something to eat or drink.

Karen Rosenblatt
Los Angeles, California

When I was a boy I used to have side aches and I wondered about them, too. I still do not know much about them, but maybe I can help a little.

Aches usually occur when muscles have worked too much and get tired or fatigued. Sometimes a muscle may also get a cramp. It tightens up and will not relax again. This is especially bad if it happens when you are swimming. A cramp in a muscle can happen in sudden vigorous exercise or sometimes when a muscle suddenly gets chilled.

Let's think a little about how a muscle works and what it needs. In its first few contractions a muscle uses up most of its immediate source of energy, a special chemical often called ATP. After that it must make more ATP. This can be done by using up another chemical called glycogen, which breaks down to lactic acid. By now the muscle needs a supply of blood to bring in oxygen and carry away some of the lactic acid.

If you are going to keep running or working hard, your muscles need a good supply of blood. If you have just eaten, a lot of your blood is being carried to the walls of your stomach and small intestine. Even though your heart pumps harder, it can't get the muscles all the blood they need. Then they are more likely to ache or get cramps. An athlete never should do any strenuous exercising soon after a meal.

An ache or pain is trying to tell you that something in your body isn't working right or that you asked it to do more than it was able to do. Physical training is a way of getting your body machinery able to work better and longer without getting aches and pains.

What does a cancer cell do to you? What color is it?

Carol Lundquist
Congers, New York

Most of the cells in the body of an animal or plant become specialized for some particular job. After that they stop growing and dividing to make more new cells. Sometimes something goes wrong and one of those cells starts growing and dividing again when it is not supposed to. We call that a cancer cell.

A cancer cell does not have any particular color. It takes a specially trained medical scientist, a pathologist, to tell a cancer cell from a normal cell.

An important practical question in biology is what makes a normal cell turn into a cancer cell. Someday, when we know enough about how normal living cells work, we hope to find an answer.

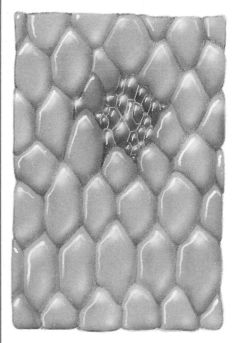

What causes someone to be an albino?

Ann-Margaret Hovsepian
Montreal, Quebec

You have noticed that one of the ways in which people differ from one another is in the amount of pigment or color of our hair and eyes and skin. All of us have the same pigment, a stuff called melanin, but we may have different amounts.

An albino is a person whose body makes no pigment at all. That is a very rare condition. It is sometimes called an inherited condition. However, an albino may have parents and grandparents who are not albinos. Just how that can happen is one of the things you will learn when you study the special part of biology called genetics.

I guess you know that albinism is not limited to the human. It can occur in most (maybe in all) wild animals. A perfectly white frog or snake or wolf is a very strange sight. An albino makes you realize how important pigments are to animals.

Do you think there is human-like life in outer space?

Francis Fletcher
Hyde Park, Massachusetts

I think this is likely, just as many other scientists do. Our Earth is a special planet of our Solar System. It gets just the right amount of light from the Sun and has temperatures and the water and atmosphere that are favorable for living things. But there are in the universe millions of other stars much like our Sun. So probably there are many planets much like our Earth in having conditions favorable for life.

No one yet knows the answer to your question. I guess yes. How do you guess?

Why do I always get shivers when someone scratches fingernails on a blackboard?

Elizabeth Wade
North Stonington, Connecticut

I can't give you a complete answer, but I will tell you what I can. Your experience is fairly common. When I was teaching it sometimes happened that the chalk I was using made a screech on the blackboard.

Then some of the students (not all of them) would groan or yell.

The sound we are talking about is high-pitched or of high frequency. I think you can sense it only by your ears. The messages from your ears to your brain use a pathway of at least four nerve fibers, which connect together at several points in the spinal cord just below the brain. It might be that some of those connections also connect to nerve fibers from lower in your spinal cord. Maybe that is how you get the shivering feeling.

I know this is not much of an explanation. This is the kind of question that even big medical books do not talk about.

How do you dream?

Julia Thompson
Arlington, Massachusetts

People have wondered about dreams for a very long time. No one knows all about them. But I can tell you a little.

Dreams are perfectly normal, and everyone seems to have them. Most of us spend 1½ to 2 hours dreaming every night. Unless we happen to wake up during a dreaming period, we do not remember our dreams.

How do we know all that? Mostly by studying people during sleep. When the brain is active, there are small electrical currents that can be detected even on the surface of your head. The pattern of electrical activity is called an electroencephalogram.

Another thing that can happen during sleep is a movement of the eyes, called REM for "rapid eye movement." It was found that the three things—dreaming, electrical activity, and REM—all go together. So you can tell when a person is dreaming without ever waking the person up.

It is believed that almost all mammals and birds also have dreams because they have periods of brain electrical activity and REM sleep.

Since dreaming is so common, scientists naturally have supposed that it is good for you. Some even think that it is something your brain needs to do.

One recent report suggests that you dream just because your brain is tuning up its electrical machinery while you are asleep. Of course, since we do not know much about how the machinery works, we don't know what tuning up means, either.

Maybe the most interesting part is that we all have dreams that we never know about. We seem to remember a dream only when we happen to wake up in the middle of one.

What is the smallest organ in the body?

Gina Quesada
Passaic, New Jersey

Technically speaking, that would be the cell. While the cell isn't an organ in our general sense of the word, it does perform many important functions on its own and as part of other organs. Just as there are billions of stars in the universe, there are billions of cells in your body.

Here's a question for you: What is the *largest* organ in the human body? You may be surprised to learn that it's the skin—something else we don't normally call an organ.

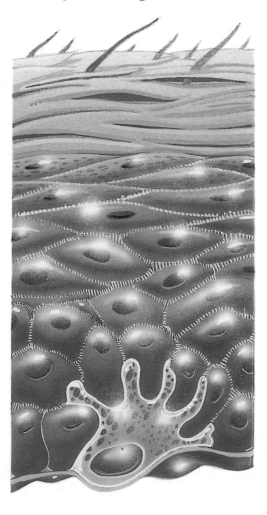

What is the use of our Adam's apple?

Karen Ross
Rockford, Illinois

What we call the Adam's apple is a swelling or projection at the front of the throat. It is larger in men than in women and is sometimes called a secondary sex characteristic. This just means that it is one of many small ways in which males are different from females.

At the upper end of your trachea (windpipe) there is an enlargement called the larynx (voice box). The larynx contains your vocal cords, which you can tighten or loosen to make different kinds of sounds, say words, and sing. A protective covering over the front of the larynx is called the thyroid cartilage. Part of the growing-up process in boys is a sudden increase in size of the larynx. The voice changes to a deeper pitch and the Adam's apple becomes more noticeable.

So the Adam's apple is the projection caused by the thick thyroid cartilage that protects the larynx.

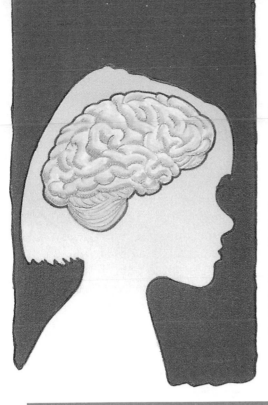

What color is the brain?

Jay McGee
Snyder, Texas

The brain is gray in color. In fact, I have heard people refer to their brains as their "gray matter."

Brains from humans and from animals have been studied very carefully. The brains of different animals differ in shape but have recognizable parts that are very much alike. When a brain is sliced in two, the brain shows some white areas deep inside surrounded by gray areas on the outside. It turns out that the white areas contain only nerve fibers. The gray areas are places where the many connections between nerve fibers are made.

All this does not tell much about how the brain does the marvelous job of thinking, but it does tell why the outside of the brain is gray.

Why are some people born handicapped?

Cynthia McIntosh
Emsworth, Pennsylvania

Since I am a physiologist I like to think of the body as a very fine and complicated machine. Our bodies are very much alike but never exactly alike. You will always be able to find someone who can do something that you can't do. Since no one has a really perfect body, I guess you could say that we are all handicapped in some way.

Some of us are more handicapped than others. And there are many ways in which this happens: in how our bones are made, in how well our hearts or brains or muscles or eyes work, and in many other ways.

147

How come you can put a lot of water in your mouth and it does not go down your throat unless you want it to?

Ben Vitulli
St. Paul, Minnesota

You are right in your observation. Neither food nor water just drops from your throat down to your stomach. You have to make that happen by swallowing.

The back of your mouth leads to your throat or pharynx, and that opens into a tube, the esophagus, that goes to your stomach. Normally the upper end of the esophagus is kept closed by a ring of muscle that acts as a valve. So water in your mouth doesn't just run down to your stomach.

Once you get some water or food at the back of your mouth, you may decide to swallow.

How come I get a runny nose when I eat hot food or drink hot drinks, even when I don't have a cold?

Brent Carlson
Norwich, Connecticut

The inside of your nose and mouth are always making a little fluid to keep the linings moist. A number of things will make them produce more fluid. Your mouth can "water," meaning that you make more fluid saliva, whenever you put food in it and sometimes when you just smell food. Your nose "waters" especially when its lining is irritated, as when you have a cold. So I suppose that your nose "waters" because its lining is especially sensitive to hot things in your mouth.

I have not noticed that my nose behaves that way, though I sometimes get tears in my eyes from eating or drinking something too hot. However, I am not surprised that your nose behaves differently than mine. Our body machinery is all basically alike, but not always exactly alike. This would be a pretty dull world if we were all exactly alike.

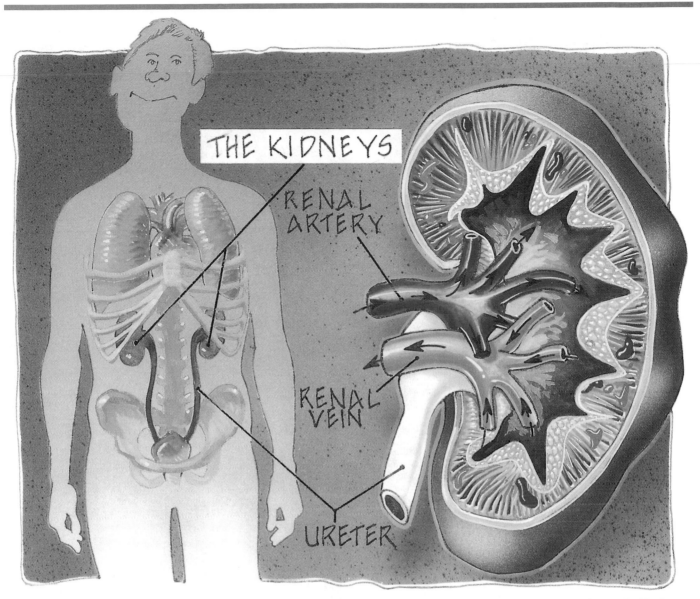

THE KIDNEYS

RENAL ARTERY

RENAL VEIN

URETER

What part of the body does the most work?

Amy Botter
Wilmer, Alabama

One reason that is hard to answer is because different parts of your body do different kinds of work. Your heart muscle and the muscles of your arms and legs do mechanical work—like the motor of an automobile. Your liver and kidneys do chemical work—like a factory that makes plastics out of petroleum. Your brain does chemical work that partly changes into the electrical work of your communication center—not too different from computers and telephone switchboards.

You need all of these, so we're not talking about which is most important. But which does the most work? One way to think about this is to ask which part gets the greatest supply of blood in relation to its size. Of course, the heart may seem greatest, but of all the blood pumped by the heart only a small part goes to the heart muscle.

The liver, the kidneys, and the brain are all big users of blood. I think that for their size the kidneys probably have the greatest blood supply.

So my vote is for the kidneys as the hardest working, but as you can see, I used a special criterion to get that answer. So if you want, you can still find reasons to argue for other organs—like the liver or heart or brain.

149

A fact is that plants need carbon dioxide from people and people need oxygen from plants. Why is it that in the car without plants you can still live?

Kelly Crane
Tampa, Florida

You are right that people and plants need each other because they trade back and forth the gases oxygen and carbon dioxide.

If you were really sealed up alone in a room so that no gases could get in or out, you would die. The air in the room would get too much carbon dioxide and lose most of its oxygen.

The reason you do not worry about this in a car is that then you really are not "sealed up." There is enough leakage of air in and out. I guess it is a good idea that cars are not more tightly made.

How does a blister form? And why is there liquid inside?

Erin Christ
Zanesville, Ohio

A blister forms at a place where you have caused damage, as by a bad pinch or a burn. A lot of sudden changes took place there. The walls of the tiny blood vessels close by became leaky. Some fluid leaked out of the blood to make the clear fluid that you see in most blisters. Sometimes the whole blood leaks out and collects to make a black-looking blister. Neither kind is any fun.

150

I'd like you to clear up something for me. Can the human eye slow down the visual speed of something that's going faster than it looks like? A few nights ago I was lying in my bed and watching the ceiling fan. It has four blades, and it was on a medium speed, where all you could see was a blur of blades. Then I started blinking very fast, and I could see the four blades. Was I imagining or not?

Anh Tran
Mustang, Oklahoma

I think you made a very interesting discovery. I think you were getting what is called a **stroboscopic** effect. To think about it, let's talk about an instrument that is called a stroboscope. This has a flash lamp, like the kind used with a camera. It gives a very short flash of light, less than one thousandth of a second long. It also has a timer to make the lamp flash again and again at some steady rate. The rate can be chosen by turning a dial to give a number from 5 to 100 or more flashes per second.

Now suppose we have a wheel that is turned by an electric motor and we want to know how fast it is turning. We make a mark near the edge of the wheel and then turn on the motor. Now we slowly increase the flashing rate of our stroboscope until we get to exactly the right rate, maybe 30 per second. We will know that we have found the right rate because then the wheel will seem to stop and the mark will seem to stay in one place. Then we will know that the motor and wheel are turning at 30 revolutions per second. Of course, part of the reason this works is that your eye keeps "seeing" for a little while after each flash. That way the effects of all the flashes just blur together.

Another way to make a stroboscope is to have a shutter that would open for very short times over and over and would be operated by a timer. Then we could shine a bright light on the wheel and look at it through the shutter. As with the flashing light, the wheel would seem to stop when we set the timer of the shutter at just the right rate.

Now I think you can see how blinking your eyes just right might work like a shutter and make the fan blades seem to stand still.

I am going to try your experiment and see if I can make it work, too. Most fans turn at high speed, and you could never blink your eyes that fast. But big old ceiling fans usually turn more slowly. I think that's why your experiment worked. Now you know how it feels to make a discovery. I would say you were thinking like a scientist.

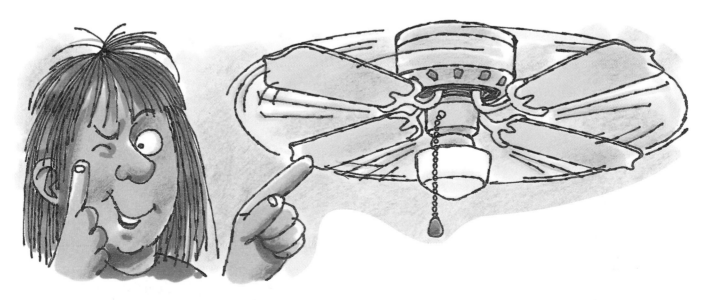

If we have two eyes, how come we don't see double?

Abby Myers
Wilkes-Barre, Pennsylvania

The direction of each of your eyes is controlled by three pairs of muscles connected to the outside of the eyeball. These are the most precisely controlled muscles of your body. They are controlled by nerve messages from the brain to keep your eyes pointed together.

Seeing begins with nerve messages sent by light-sensitive cells in the retina at the back of each eye and ending up in your brain. That all works so that your brain "sees" a picture of the little image that falls on the retina. And the eyes are pointed together so carefully that the same picture is formed by messages from your two eyes. That's how you can use two eyes to see "single" and not "double."

When you open your eyes wide, why do your pupils become smaller?

L. Smith
Hammond, Lousisiana

I tried that in front of a mirror, and I think it works just as you say. For me, it's much easier to see if I put up a hand to partly shade my eyes. If I shade them so that less light falls on my eyes, the pupils get bigger. Then, if I take my hand away so that more light falls on my eyes, the pupils get smaller.

The pupil of your eye is the little black spot in the center of the colored circle. The pupil is the window of your eye, the only place where light can get in. The colored circle around it is called the iris. It is a little circular sheet of muscle that can make the pupil larger or smaller. The iris muscle is controlled by nerves that connect to give a neat reflex action, the kind of nerve control you never think about. That way the iris works automatically to regulate the size of the pupil and the amount of light that it lets into your eyes.

You can see all this happen by looking at your own eyes in a well-lighted mirror.

Why do people have moles on their skin?

Charity Hunt
Ava, Missouri

Although most of us do not think very much about our skin, we are fortunate to have such a good protective layer. The skin actually has a number of layers, all very carefully arranged, together with some hair follicles and some little glands that make oil and some that make sweat. One of the underneath layers is made of cells with a pigment that gives the skin its color.

A mole is a small, colored patch of skin where the layers somehow got mixed up and there are a lot of extra pigment cells. Most moles never cause any trouble, and we just live with them. If a mole bleeds or grows or changes in color, then it is wise to show it to a doctor. Removing a mole is a small operation and should be done only by a doctor.

Almost everyone has a few moles. Most moles are a part of us from birth. I think of mine as small accidents that occurred when I was becoming a baby.

153

I like science and want to be a scientist when I grow up. But I don't know the things that will make me one. Can you help?

David Kuric
Vista, California

There isn't one special answer that will work for everyone, but I can give you some ideas. Start with a particular part of nature—the world around you—that you can learn about and understand.

Here are some suggestions. How about birds? Ask your mom or dad if you can put up a bird feeder. Then try to find someone in your neighborhood who is a bird watcher and can teach you about the birds.

How about numbers? You may think that addition and subtraction and fractions are pretty dull. But you will be surprised if you start doing puzzles and games with them. Numbers can be fun.

How about stars? Look for someone in your neighborhood who can help you pick out stars and constellations.

There are lots of ideas like these that will be fun and teach you things you will never learn from books. Books are not science. They only help you understand it.

154

How do some people get to be scientists?

Julie Morgan
Rockford, Illinois

I do not know anyone who has all of the answers to this question, but I will tell you my ideas about it. The first idea is that people who become scientists are curious people. They wonder about the universe, or the world we live in, or about its people. And they wonder hard enough to want to find out. They like puzzles; they like to solve problems. In fact, they like to think.

A famous scientist, a physicist who worked at the Bell Laboratories, once asked me, "How many people ever really sit and think?" What he meant was that many people do not like questions unless someone else tells them the answers, or maybe he meant that many people are lazy in using their brains. I think that lazy-brain people would never become scientists.

Of course, no one will ever learn much about science just sitting on a desert island and thinking. We need to know the ideas about science that already are known, the ones that scientists before us have discovered. Galileo, who lived about 400 years ago, was one of the great scientists of all time. If you are in the fifth grade, you already know a great deal more about our world than Galileo did.

We also need to learn how to use the tools of science. Some tools are instruments, like microscopes or telescopes or computers. Learning to use them is a little like learning to drive a car. Some tools are just ways of thinking—like mathematics. Of course, mathematics is a special kind of science all by itself. But for most scientists, mathematics is their most powerful tool.

So if you have an idea that you might like to be a scientist, one bit of advice anyone will give is to study math. For some of us math is easy; for some of us it's hard. And when it is hard, it usually also seems dull. I was very poor in math until the eighth grade. I don't remember exactly what happened, but somehow I solved a problem all by myself. And suddenly I thought, "Gee, that was fun." After that I liked math, and I have learned to use it in my work, even though I never really got to be a good mathematician.

Suppose you work hard to learn about science and math and then later decide you don't want to be a scientist. Should you worry about that? Will your study be wasted? I don't think so. We live in a world that depends upon science and technology. The more you know about science, the more you will feel at home in the world you are growing up in.

155

Do you have to be smart to become a scientist?

Jennifer Pineda
Los Angeles, California

I don't know about that word *smart* that you used. A scientist must be able to learn and keep learning, because in science there is always more to learn. And a scientist must do a lot of thinking. Just memorizing isn't good enough.

And a scientist needs an imagination. After you have learned a lot about a subject and thought about it, you need to wonder: why are there so many things we do not know about it?

I guess you could say that being a scientist takes a lot of head work.

Are there any diseases that once didn't exist at all but exist now?

Susan Dalgarn
Saginaw, Michigan

There are different kinds of diseases, but you must be thinking of illnesses caused by microbes, such as measles, chicken pox, and pneumonia.

I think the answer to your question is yes. It is just too hard for me to imagine that the first humans had all the same diseases we have today. But it's also true that we have no record of a disease that suddenly came "out of nowhere."

Disease always involves two different organisms. There is the parasite (a microbe) and the host (in this case, a person). Most of us carry parasitic microbes that don't hurt us. Parasites usually need to grow inside the body before they can cause diseases. And our bodies have defenses to keep this from happening.

One disease that we've heard about for only ten years or so is AIDS. It is believed to have originated in Africa, where the AIDS microbe was just a "quiet" parasite. Evidently, something changed to make it able to cause a serious disease. You can argue both ways about whether it is or is not a "new" disease. I suspect that if we could track any disease back to its origin, we would have the same kind of problem.

Questions About the World

Why is it that if you drop an object into water, it falls quickly until it hits the water?

Jill Kress
Pittsburgh, Pennsylvania

You are quite right about your observation. You can feel it happen every time you dive into a swimming pool. You suddenly slow down when you hit the water.

You are talking about an interesting property of fluids. Both air and water are fluids because both of them can flow. Some fluids flow more easily than others. Air flows more easily than water. (And water flows more easily than pancake syrup.)

When you are diving through air, the air is pushed to the side and must flow around you. It's so easy that it only feels like wind going by. Once you hit the water, however, the water must flow around you. And water does not flow so easily. That's what slows you down.

I have never dived into pancake syrup, but I think I wouldn't want to. That would really slow you down.

Whenever I get my hair wet, it is darker than when it is dry. Why?

Jane Boyer
Festus, Missouri

Many things are darker when wet. Garden soil is, and paper is, too. I was surprised how much darker white Kleenex is when you make a wet spot on it.

If something gets darker, that means it is reflecting less light to your eye. Evidently a wet surface tends to trap light better and doesn't bounce it off as well. I think that may be why your hair looks darker when wet.

What makes stars shine and sometimes blink?

Karla Lindula
Auburn, Washington

We think that stars shine because each of them is a big hot glowing ball of gas like our sun. So just think of stars as suns—but very much farther away.

That twinkle does not come from the star itself. Light from the star comes to our eyes through a thick layer of air around our earth. Light goes right through that air layer, but it gets twisted back and forth just a little as it goes through winds and hot and cold layers up there. So the little beam of light from a star gets jumbled enough to make the star seem to twinkle.

That twinkling is a big problem for astronomers. You can see why they put their telescopes on high mountains so they do not have to look through such a thick layer of air.

Would you please explain why the so-called Jack Frost pictures and designs get to be on our windows?

Laurie Ann Boast
Noranda, Quebec

You can see that the frost on a window is always on the inside. And if the outside temperature warms up, or maybe if a window is right in the sun, the frost may melt into water that runs down on the inside of the window. So, you can see that the frost is made out of ice that formed on the inside of the window.

Frost forms on a window when the temperature outside is below freezing. Inside it is warmer, and there is more water vapor in the air. Any water molecule in the air that hits the glass will stick to the surface. As it sticks, it is hooking up to other water molecules to form ice crystals.

Every water molecule is made of one oxygen and two hydrogen atoms, H-O-H. Water molecules can stick together by sharing their hydrogen atoms. They tend to make six-sided shapes but in all kinds of patterns. The really amazing thing about frost on windows is that it forms in such varied and beautiful patterns. If you were wondering why they make some of the particular Jack Frost patterns, I just have to say that I do not know.

I have been thinking that Jack Frost patterns on windows must be common where you live in Canada. That led me to think also that some people have never seen them.

159

I have a question for you. We live by a lake. My sister, Melissa, and I have been skating on it several times. We have heard strange noises coming from the lake when it is frozen. It happened right under me once! We can also hear them from our house. They are very loud. Can you tell me what they are?

Michelle Wang
Germantown, Maryland

If the noises you hear are like sharp cracks with some rumblings, I think they are made by the ice. As you know, ice expands as it freezes. That's what makes it float. That also tends to squeeze the ice outward. As ice freezes and thaws and freezes again, it does all sorts of pushing and shoving that makes it crack and rumble. You can play that it is talking to you.

Why is the sky blue, and what makes it?

Melissa Martin
Satsuma, Alabama

The sky is blue because of the small scattering of sunlight by molecules of gases in the air, mostly by nitrogen molecules. We think of air as being clear and transparent—and it is. We think of sunlight as being almost white—and it is.

But in going thousands of miles through our atmosphere, a tiny amount of sunlight is scattered. When that happens, blue light rays are scattered more than red light rays—in fact, about six times more. So, the light that is scattered down to us from the sky looks blue. I'm glad that happens. If it did not, the sky would look black.

I live in the Bay Area and lately we've had quite a few earthquakes. I am 11 years old, and this worries me. It is scary. Please help.

Laura Caeton
Fremont, California

I am glad that you wrote me. Whenever something is bugging you, it is much better to talk about it than to keep it bottled up inside.

I cannot do anything to help if you mean stopping earthquakes. But maybe I can say some things that will help you to think about the problem.

I suppose that people in your area talk about earthquakes a lot. Every place seems to have its own special problems. Where I live in Texas, people worry about tornadoes. So, we often get warnings on TV that there is a "tornado watch in our area until 10 o'clock tonight." When a tornado hits a house, it just about takes everything away, so it is pretty scary. People who lived along the Gulf Coast worry about hurricanes. Almost every year a hurricane clobbers some part of the coast. Hurricanes are scary, too.

Some people live where there are floods. They could worry about being drowned or losing their homes just because a river nearby gets too much rain.

I guess I am trying to think of other people who have scary things that might happen to them. There are a lot more we could think of. Actually, all those things put together probably do not hurt as many people as are hurt in automobile accidents. I guess just living is a little bit risky because of the many things that can go wrong. But living is not as risky as it used to be. People are a lot safer and live longer than they used to do.

When my first daughter, Shirley, was a little girl, I got to thinking about all the dangers and all the ways she could get hurt. Finally, I wondered how kids ever could live to grow up. Then I realized that most kids do grow up in spite of all the things that can happen. I decided that worrying would not help any. So, I decided to be sensible and careful—like always wearing seat belts in a car and just expect that everything will come out all right.

So, why don't you try my idea and see if it will work?

Will you please explain to me how the back cover of a matchbook is attracted to the tip of a match to make fire?

Kim Meredith
Newark, New Jersey

You are right that it takes both the tip of the match and a special surface to make fire.

However, the two do not attract each other. The match tip must be rubbed on the striking surface.

The idea is the same as the Indian way of making a fire by rubbing two sticks together next to some easy-to-burn stuff like fine wood shavings. We need something that gets hot by friction and something easy to burn. Chemists found things much easier to burn and invented matches that start to burn with only a little friction.

The head of a safety match usually has a chemical called potassium chlorate and some charcoal or sulfur. The striking surface has some red phosphorous and fine sand. That combination lights easily, so it does not take much rubbing to make the match tip start to burn.

Of course, anything that easy to burn ought to be handled carefully. It is easy to get fingers burned by careless use of matches.

How does fire get its colors?

Emily Glenn
Delaware, Ohio

Most things that burn contain the element carbon. It burns by combining with oxygen to make carbon dioxide. But almost always some of the carbon is not completely burned and comes off as a black smoke. While the carbon particles are in the hot flame, they give a yellow glow. So, most fires are yellow.

For some things, like burning wood, other colors besides yellow may appear in the flames. I think they come mostly from minerals in the wood. Although they do not burn, some metals give off special colors when they get hot. In fact, color in a flame is used by chemists as tests for some metals. I will make a list of a few elements with their colors in a flame:

sodium—yellow
potassium—violet
copper—green
strontium—red

I think some of these are also used to give the special colors in fireworks.

How does fire turn into ash after it burns?

Anne Tegtmeier
Arvado, Colorado

I think the fire itself, the flame, does not turn into ash. It may seem to you almost the same thing if I say that ash is left after a fire has burned. Or, we could say that fire can turn wood into ash. Actually, the ash is stuff that was there in the wood to start with, a small part of the wood that the fire could not burn.

Except for gasoline and natural gas, most of the things we burn leave some ash. Ash comes from minerals. The ash left by burning wood comes from minerals that a tree needed and took up from the soil by its roots.

163

I was wondering, if seedless grapes don't have seeds, how do they grow?

Cathy Clem
Suffolk, Virginia

I suppose you are thinking that plants grow up from seeds. And you are right. You can't get seedless grapes that way if they don't make seeds.

Many kinds of plants also can reproduce in a different way. Some part of the plant, usually a piece of the stem, is planted in the soil. It will first grow roots and then grow into a complete plant. I believe that all kinds of grapes are grown in this way.

You might like to try this idea by cutting a small section of leaves and stems from an ivy plant. Just put it in a glass of water some place in your room where it will get some light.

Be patient. Nothing will happen overnight. In time your ivy stem should begin growing roots.

What causes the seed, after the sun has shone and the rain has poured, to pop up into a plant?

Emma Chanlett-Avery
Hinton, West Virginia

A seed is already a tiny plant, an embryo all ready to grow. It also has stored food material to live on until it can put out green leaves and make its own food. And it usually has a tough outer coat to protect it until it is time to grow.

How does a seed know when it is time to grow? First, something must happen inside to get the embryo ready. Most seeds need to wait until the next spring before they start to grow. Some have to just wait, some need to get cold, some need to dry out before they are ready. After that, almost all seeds need the same things to start growing: water and warmth. So, that's why you see little plants popping up from seeds on a warm spring day after a rain.

We have an oak tree in our backyard (the reason we know that it is oak is because of its acorns). The leaves used to look like this . Now they look like this  and this year they started to look like this ! Can you explain this?

Joseph Miller
Virginia Beach, Virginia

I think you were very observant. Not many people would have noticed. And not many would have made sure it was an oak tree by its acorns.

Anyone who has spent much time looking at trees learns to recognize different kinds by the shapes of their leaves. The maple leaf is so distinctive that Canada has made it a national symbol. So we are used to the idea that each kind of tree makes its leaves in one special shape.

Now it is also true that some trees are a bit careless in making leaves. It just happens that oaks are good examples of trees that may make their leaves in patterns that are not always the same. Another example is poison ivy, which is usually a bush rather than a tree, but also does not always have exactly the same patterns for its leaves.

If you study any one kind of plant or animal, you soon discover that individuals are all alike in some ways but different in others.

It's easy to see that this is true about human beings. Wouldn't it be terrible if we were all exactly alike?

I would like to know what makes volcanoes come out of the ground. I am interested in this.

Stuart Beck
Commack, New York

Not all volcanoes are alike. Probably you are thinking about the kind that come out of the tops of mountains. Usually the whole mountain was formed by hot liquid stuff that came out of the volcano, flowed down the sides, and hardened into rock. Then we may call that whole mountain a volcano.

Sometimes volcanoes are called "windows into the earth." They tell us that way down deep the earth has a very hot and liquid core. The part of the earth where we live is the solid crust on the outside.

The hot liquid stuff of the core is called magma. It is under great pressure from the crust above. At some place where the crust is weaker, magma may be forced upward, melting rocks of the crust with its great heat. The melting rocks release gases that make the magma push upward still more.

All that bubbly hot magma tries to get out through the crust. Sometimes it quietly bubbles upward through a hole in the mountain and flows down the sides. Sometimes it is partly blocked and then builds up pressure until it violently erupts.

Volcanoes behave in different ways—some quietly, some violently. All of them are formed by the hot liquid magma that is usually deep below us in the earth.

I would like to know what causes an earthquake?

Stacey Sookerskoff
Saskatoon, Saskatchewan

We live on the outer crust, the wrinkled outside skin, of the earth. We think that the earth is very steady, and most of the time and in most places it is. But down underneath, slow movements are going on. If the crust were nice and flexible, it would move slowly, too—so slowly that we would not notice it.

Where the crust of the earth is very rigid and where slow movements are occurring underneath, then the crust may crack and slip a little. That makes an earthquake.

How do volcanoes affect the weather?

Christy Van Dyke
Kansas City, Kansas

The eruption of a volcano affects our weather mostly by the big cloud of dust that it sends high up into the air. At first the dust cloud may darken the earth for miles around the volcano. Then the cloud gradually gets thinner as it is mixed up by winds.

A very large cloud of dust came from the eruption of the volcano El Chichon in southern Mexico in April 1982. This was big enough to be seen in photos taken by our satellites. The cloud rose to a height of about 15 miles. There, a wind stream carried it in a narrow path all the way around the earth. Parts of the cloud could still be seen in photos three weeks later.

So far I have not seen any report about special effects of that dust cloud on our weather. Some effects are certain to have happened somewhere, just because a dust cloud reflects sunlight and will cause at least a small local, cooling effect. But weather is so variable anyway that some small effect is often difficult to see.

167

Could you give me some information about auroras?

Renee Leach
Baltimore, Maryland

An aurora is a wavering glow of light that is seen sometimes in the night sky in the direction of the North or South poles. The ones we see in the Northern Hemisphere are sometimes also called the northern lights.

An aurora is caused by very fast, charged particles—mostly electrons—that came from the Sun. Because of the earth's magnetic field, these are partially deflected so that they come into our atmosphere toward the North and South poles. When nitrogen molecules of our air are hit by those fast particles, they become very excited molecules.

They become ordinary molecules again by giving off energy as light. That gives the faint wavering glow we call an aurora.

I have little stickers that glow in the dark after the light goes off. How do they do that?

Christopher Dial
Talent, Oregon

There are a number of chemicals that are special in the way they react with light. They have molecules that take up light particles, or photons. They become "excited" molecules because they are holding extra energy that came from the photons. Later in time, they lose their "excitement" by giving off photons. Then they are giving off light and glowing.

For some molecules, photons are given off very quickly, even in billionths of a second. Such a very fast glow is called **fluorescence**. Some molecules hold on to their photon energy for a much longer time, even for hours. That slow glow is often called **phosphorescence**. You can see that fast and slow glows are much alike. Your stickers must contain some phosphorescent material.

One place that's easy to see phosphorescence is in a fluorescent lamp. It works mostly by a very fast glow of chemicals on the inside of the glass. But some of those chemicals also have a slow glow. A way to see this is to watch a fluorescent lamp in a dark room as you flip the light switch to turn it off. You will see that it glows a little after you turn off the switch.

168

What makes it snow?

Stephanie Waters
Indiantown, Florida

Snow forms in clouds when the air temperature up there gets below freezing. Water molecules come out of the air and stick together in special patterns of little ice crystals. Then the ice crystals keep getting bigger or tangle up in little clumps to form snowflakes.

Snowflakes have very intricate crystal patterns. There was a scientist who learned how to catch snowflakes and keep them cold long enough to take photographs. He photographed more than a thousand snowflakes without finding any two that were exactly alike. The scientist was called "Snowflake" Bentley.

Now that you know what snow is made of, let's hope we don't see too much of it at any one time.

How come snow is white?

Susannah Elwyn
Horseheads, New York

Why is snow white? The technical answer is that snow reflects most of the light that falls on it and it reflects all colors equally. You know that liquid water is clear and so nearly colorless that you can look right through it. That's also true of ice if it is made from pure water and has no cracks. If you scrape some ice, maybe with a knife or with your skates, you will see that scrapings are white and look something like snow. Just as with scraped ice, snow crystals scatter light rays and bounce them back without absorbing much. Since the snow doesn't absorb any color, we say that it is white.

How does a compass know where to point? How does it know the right direction?

Jennifer Pineda
Quartz Hill, California

A compass, as you know, has a small needle-like magnet for a pointer. Because the earth is a big magnet, the pointer-magnet of a compass lines up with the earth's magnetic field. So, the needle points almost north and south.

However, the earth's magnetic north pole is not exactly at the true North Pole. There are also small changes from place to place in the magnetic declination, how far off the compass will be from pointing true north.

If you want to know how to correct the compass in your area, I suggest you ask your local surveyor. He can tell you the proper declination to use.

In winter, every morning I look out the window and it's foggy. What causes that?

Timothy Manglona
San Diego, California

Fog forms when moist air is cooled a little. Then the water vapor condenses to make the many tiny droplets of water.

In some places the special conditions needed to make fog are likely to occur at certain times of year.

You live in San Diego, near the Pacific coast. I think your fogs occur when warm moist air from the ocean blows in over cooler water near shore.

I can't understand why clouds are white.

Jon Miller
Krum, Texas

It happens that I wrote an answer to that question when I answered Susannah Elwyn, who asked why snow is white. When I wrote Susannah's answer, I was not thinking about clouds, but clouds and snow are white for the same reason. They reflect most of the light that falls on them, and they reflect all colors equally.

What makes it rain?

Kim Scott
Snellville, Georgia

Rain always comes from a cloud. But, as you know, something special must happen in a cloud to make rain. Most clouds are made of water droplets so small that they are easily held up by very weak air currents.

In order to make rain, something has to happen to collect many tiny droplets into big drops, big enough to fall. One way this can happen is when there is a strong updraft. As it rises, the air expands and cools. In the churning air near the top of the cloud there are lots of collisions between droplets. Bigger droplets keep picking up smaller ones until they become raindrops big enough to fall.

Sometimes, if it gets cold enough in the cloud, ice crystals form. If they grow big enough to fall, they collect water droplets and may melt on the way down.

A lot has to happen up there in a cloud to make rain. Something has to turn many tiny floating droplets into large falling raindrops.

171

How does the oil on water change different colors like a rainbow? Is it because of the light reflections? Could you please explain it?

Courtney Pavelka
Denver, Colorado

That is an interesting sight that almost everyone sees sometime. An oil layer on water may spread out until it is very thin. When it gets to a particular thinness (or thickness), something special happens.

The water surface acts partly like a mirror and reflects back some of the light falling on it. An added oil layer now gives two partial mirrors very close together. When the distance between the mirrors is the same as the wave length of light, then those light waves cancel each other out. Then you see all the other wave lengths. Different wave lengths of light have different colors. So, you can say that the thin double mirror of an oil film on water actually erases some colors and leaves the others for you to see.

Sometimes I see a large, rainbow-like ring around the Moon and Sun. What causes this ring? I've been wondering for some time now.

Kathy Sue Brown
San Diego, California

That ring is sometimes called a halo. It is believed to be caused by the scattering of sunlight by tiny ice crystals very high in the sky.

High clouds of ice crystals high in the sky are called cirrus clouds, or cirrostratus if they form a layer. These often form in front of warm fronts that bring rain.

So, a halo around the Sun or Moon is often a warning that rain may come.

172

This afternoon I looked up and saw a rainbow moving back and forth across the wall. My mom said the sun goes to the fish tank and the sun in the fish tank goes to the wall. I don't believe her. What really happened?

Erica Martin
Tempe, Arizona

I think your mother is right. Here is what probably happened. A narrow band or sunlight fell upon your fish tank near one corner. Then the glass and water acted like a prism to break up the white light of sunlight into its colors.

I will show you by a diagram what a prism does. You can see how a corner of your fish tank could have done the same thing. I am sure you have noticed by now that everything has to be just right with the sun at a special angle to make a corner of your fish tank act like a prism.

It takes a little while to get used to the idea that you get from the rainbow of colors made by a prism. It shows you that white light is white because it contains all colors.

What makes the Sun and Moon shine?

Julie Blackwell
Bemis, Tennessee

Isn't it funny how we take such things for granted without ever knowing what causes them?

The Sun shines with its own energy. The light you see (and feel as heat) is given off by the Sun's surface, called the **photosphere**, which is several hundred miles thick and composed of ever-changing gases. Some of the energy the Sun produces must escape, or it would build up and explode. Whenever you see the Sun shining, you'll know it's just releasing excess energy and giving us a little light and warmth in the bargain.

Remember, you should never look directly at the Sun. The light is too bright for our eyes to take.

You also asked about moonshine. The Moon gives off no light of its own but reflects sunlight from its rocky surface. What we call moonshine is actually sunshine reflected by the Moon.

Did you know that there's also a third kind of shine? It's called earthshine, meaning sunlight reflected by the Earth. We have only one way to see it. That occurs because some of the earthshine falls on the Moon and is reflected back to Earth again. By this dim light we can sometimes see the outline of the whole moon behind the crescent of a new moon.

Why is the Moon dark when it moves in front of the Sun during an eclipse?

Tracy Stevens
Poquoson, Virginia

You see an eclipse of the Sun only at some special time when the Moon gets between the Sun and the place where you are standing on Earth. Then you are in the Moon's shadow.

If you think about this some more, you will see that the back side of the Moon, the side toward you, will also be in the same shadow. So, it will always look dark.

174

Why is there a leap year every four years?

Kecia Sinclair
St. Albans, New York

Your question got me thinking about how complicated the calendar really is. Maybe you would like to think about this, too.

Our Earth travels around the Sun in a very steady way. We use that to measure time in days.

Our Earth has another regular motion in its orbit around the Sun. Along with this motion we get the seasons of the year, which repeat themselves over and over. So, we also like to think in longer time periods measured in years.

It's easy to see why people chose days and years to keep time. But right away they had a problem because the number of days in a year does not come out even. There are about 365¼ days in a year.

Now you can see the idea of a leap year, which was invented way back at the time of Julius Caesar. If we put in one extra day every four years, that will keep us about even.

Actually, adding leap years is not a perfect solution. A real year is about 11 minutes and 14 seconds shorter than 365 1/4 days. Do you know how our calendar solves this problem? If you don't, try finding out in your school library. Look up calendars. And you may also be amazed to discover how many different calendars the different peoples of the world have invented.

Every year in the calendar a day starts on another space. For example, in 1983 the month of January started on a Sunday. In 1984 it started on a Monday. How come? Also, if one year January started on Saturday, on what day would January start on next year?

Erika Munos
West New York, New Jersey

Our calendar came about through many centuries of trying to find the best system. The ideas that went into it have been traced back to the ancient Egyptians, Mesopotamians, and Romans. The Mesopotamians may have been the ones who decided that the week should have seven days.

Our week still has seven days. And, as you know, our year has 365 days (except 366 days in leap years). If you divide 7 days into 365 days, you get 52 weeks in a year with *one day left over*. So, if January 1983 started on a Sunday, then January 1984 must have begun one day later—on Monday.

Now here's a question for you. 1984 was a leap year. So what day of the week did January 1985 begin on?

Why are there constellations?

Michelle Trautman
Scotts Valley, California

I'm not just sure how to answer your question. You did not ask why there are stars. Really, I think you want to know why people invented certain patterns out of the stars that we know as constellations.

A few thousand years ago life was a lot simpler. People generally lived by the Sun and worked during the daylight hours. At night lighting by candles or oil lamps was expensive. I suppose that people spent many evenings talking with their friends.

One of the ways to pass the time at night is to look at the stars. If you look at the night sky long enough, you can easily imagine that the star patterns look like the figures of animals or people. And if you let your imagination run, you can make up stories about them. I think that's how the constellations got their names.

We know that most of the star patterns came to be named as constellations. Those same names have been used for several thousands of years.

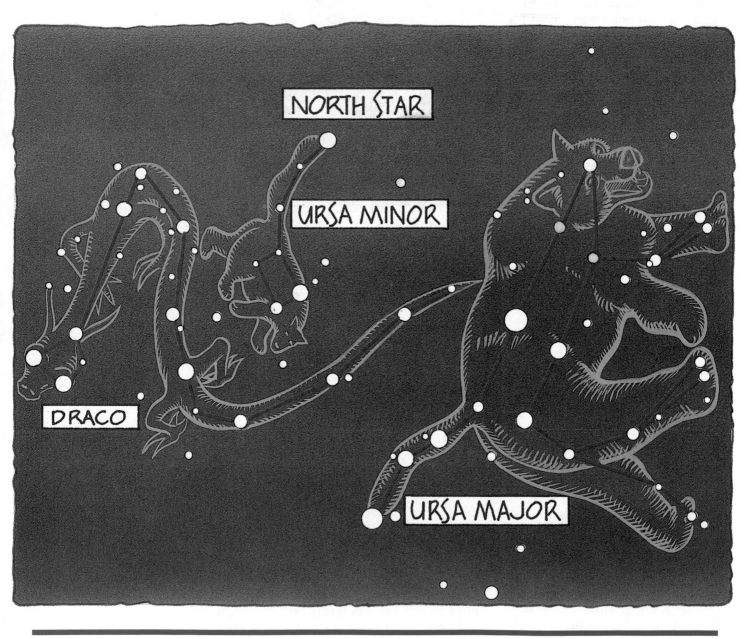

NORTH STAR

URSA MINOR

DRACO

URSA MAJOR

At night in the summer I look up at the stars and wonder what they are made of. I just keep wondering what they are made of. Could you please help me find out?

Rebecca Surratt
Atlanta, Texas

The stars are very great balls of very hot gas, mostly hydrogen and helium. Most of them are very much like our Sun.

So, when you look up at the stars at night, you can think of them as many suns looking so small because they are so far away.

How can we tell the temperature of stars?

Douglas Licerio
Palawan, Philippines

When we heat up something until it glows, we often say that it gets "red-hot." If we can make it still hotter, its color changes toward yellow, and still hotter, it becomes bluish white. So, you can see how we can tell about the temperature of something that glows like a star.

I found actual estimates of some star temperatures, given in the Centigrade temperature scale. Some of the bluish stars are about 40,000 degrees, and some of the reddish stars are only about 2,000 degrees. Our Sun is about 5,800 degrees. Of course, these are temperatures at the surface, which is the only part we can see.

177

What do aliens from outer space look like?

Hank Williams, Jr.
Kokomo, Indiana

Let me help you think about your question. There may be some kind of life in other solar systems. However, if by outer space you mean within our solar system, I think you should know that scientists conclude there is not intelligent life with that system. There are people who wonder, of course, if other solar systems may have life and if that life might be similar to humans on planet Earth. We just don't know. It would be fun to think about what that life might look like. If you thought about humans and had a chance to start over, how would *you* make them different? Might there be some intelligent life that lived totally underwater? Or that could fly?

Lots of imaginative people draw pictures of aliens from outer space. You have seen some of these on TV and in magazines. These creatures are just people's guesses from within their imagination. What would your pictures look like?

Why isn't there any air on the Moon?

Cassidy Wald
Red Deer, Alberta

That's a good question. We don't know exactly how the Moon was formed, but its composition, the stuff that makes it up, seems to be like that of the Earth. So, why no atmosphere?

The answer is that the Moon just doesn't have enough gravity to hold onto an atmosphere. Its force of gravity is only about one-ninth of that on Earth.

The force of gravity of the Earth is great enough to hold onto the gases of our atmosphere—except for the very lightest gases, hydrogen and helium. At the upper part of the Earth's atmosphere some of these two gases are continually being lost into space. So there are only tiny amounts of them left.

The Moon's gravity isn't great enough to hold any of the common gases. So, it's just a big naked ball out there without any atmosphere for clothes.

I understand the meteors are pieces of metal that fly through space. But what I don't understand is how the metal gets into space. Could you explain that?

Joshua Graml
Langley AFB, Virginia

It seems that there are many little pieces of stone or metal that keep raining down on the Earth from out in space. They come down at very high speeds and get very hot as they are slowed by the friction of the atmosphere. They get hot enough to glow. Those that are big enough, maybe the size of a pea, make a trail of light that we call a **meteor**, or shooting star. Some of the larger pieces fall all the way to earth, and some are later found as pieces of metal or stone. These are called **meteorites**.

There really are many such particles that keep coming down all the time. Anyone who patiently watches the dark sky for several hours at night (and is away from city lights) should see several shooting stars. And sometimes there are so many that they are called meteor showers. Some are believed to come from stray pieces left over from comets. There are several different ideas about just where the larger ones come from, but they are believed to be pieces that belong to our solar system.

I guess that a lot of junk must be floating around out there in space.

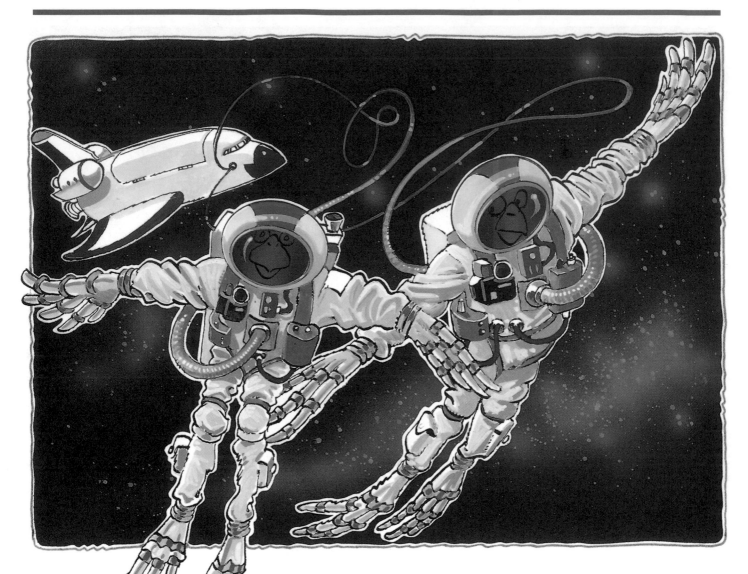

Why don't birds fly into space?

Meghan Chase
Casselberry, Florida

Your question starts from a correct idea. Birds do not fly out into space. In fact, I think it is safe to say that, in all the millions of years our Earth has had birds, we have never lost a bird that way.

So, there must be a very powerful reason why that cannot happen. Actually, there are several reasons. Let's think about two.

Some birds can fly pretty high up. I was surprised to read that some can fly as high as four miles above the earth. I am surprised because at that height the air is very thin. There are only half as many oxygen molecules in each breath of air. So, breathing is hard to do. Of course, airplanes carry people higher than that every day. But they have air pumps to pressurize the plane's cabin so that breathing feels just like it does on the ground.

Now you can see one problem. As a bird flies higher, the air gets thinner. A bird will run out of oxygen long before it gets out into space. And if a bird can't breathe, it can't fly.

There is also a second reason. In order for anything to really "escape" from the earth and get out into space, it needs a very great push in order to get up enough speed. The magic speed needed is called the escape velocity. It is about 25,000 miles per hour. You know that is a lot faster than a bird can fly.

This might seem difficult, but does sound travel in space?

Rachelle Theisen
Fargo, North Dakota

Sound is carried as a wave of compression in some material. The sounds we usually hear are carried by air.

Space is close to a perfect vacuum, meaning there's almost nothing there. So, sound does not travel in space. There is no sense in yelling at a star.

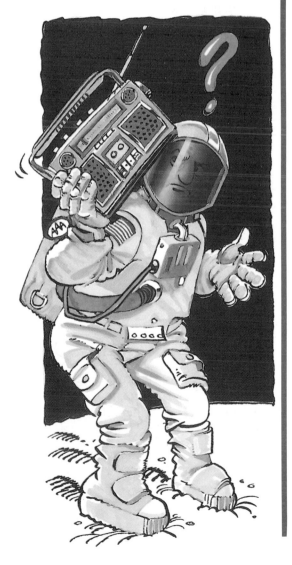

I know that there is another planet out there, but I don't know about it. Do you know anything about it?

Michelle Niehaus
Cincinnati, Ohio

The last planet to be discovered was Pluto. That happened in 1930. Astronomers had been looking for it for a long time. The reason to suspect another planet was that there were small changes in the orbits of Uranus and Neptune that could have been caused by the effect of gravity of an unknown planet.

Lately I have noticed questions about whether the mass of Pluto is really great enough to cause those effects on Uranus and Neptune. So, maybe it is possible that there is still another planet way out on the edge of our solar system. Most astronomers, it seems, don't believe that, but I guess we'll just have to wait and see.

Which is faster, heat or cold?

Sandy Wolf
Orlando, Florida

When we talk about things around us, we commonly say that something (like boiling water) is hot and something else (like an ice cube) is cold. Sometimes we even use a thermometer that measures in degrees how hot or cold something is.

When we want to think about making something hot, we can think about adding *heat* to it or taking *cold* away from it. Really, those two ways of

thinking would be exactly the same. So, the answer to your question would be: heat is just as fast as cold.

Actually, we do not use the ideas of cold in this way. All we need to think about is heat. We make something hot by adding heat. That's what a fire can do. We make something cold by taking heat away from it. That's what a refrigerator can do.

A lot of different conditions affect how fast you can add heat to make something hot. They work in just the same way to affect how fast you can take heat away to make something cold.

How's that for a hot idea?

How does temperature change?

Kimmy Jones
Coon Rapids, Minnesota

Our Earth is warmed by the Sun. But it is not warmed evenly. We have some places, like the poles, that get the least sunshine and are always cold. And we have a big central band near the equator that gets the most sunshine and is usually hot. With air rising where it is hot and settling down where it is cool, there are bound to be winds in between. With things like oceans and land and lakes and mountains in between, the winds get mixed up a lot. Wherever we are, the winds do not always come from the same place. So, the temperature of the air around us can change a great deal.

We have learned a lot about our weather by studying the movement of air. The scientists who do that are called meteorologists. They usually can tell pretty well what the weather will be like. But they are never quite certain because it is hard to tell just how the winds will blow tomorrow.

How come light is so hot?

*Rhona Seidman
Silver Spring, Maryland*

Light is a form of energy very different from heat. Light itself is not hot. However, we can *make* light with something that is hot enough. And we can use light to warm something and *make* heat. So, I can see why you might have asked your question.

Of all the ways to make light, the oldest is to get something very hot. When Edison started out to make an electric light bulb, that's the idea he used. He used electricity to heat a wire sealed up in a bulb. We still use that kind of light bulb. The outer bulb gets hot, but the wire inside is heated up much hotter—to almost 3000° F. However, there are other ways to make light without much heat. Our fluorescent lamps are warm but never really get hot. And a firefly makes "cold" light—no heat at all.

We are fortunate that light can be turned into heat and used to warm something. If it were not for sunlight, our Earth would be a frozen, lifeless planet. No heat travels across that 93,000,000 miles from the Sun. It is sunlight turned into heat that keeps us warm.

Just think of light and heat as different forms of energy that can be changed from one to the other.

I read that everything expands when it's heated. Would it shrink when it gets cold?

*Randy Powell
Elmore City, Oklahoma*

You are right that most things expand when they are heated. They also shrink when they get cold. So, we ought to be able to use this idea to tell what temperature it is.

That's what a thermometer does. The liquid inside expands up the tube at higher temperature and shrinks back down the tube at lower temperature. And it will keep on doing this day after day and year after year.

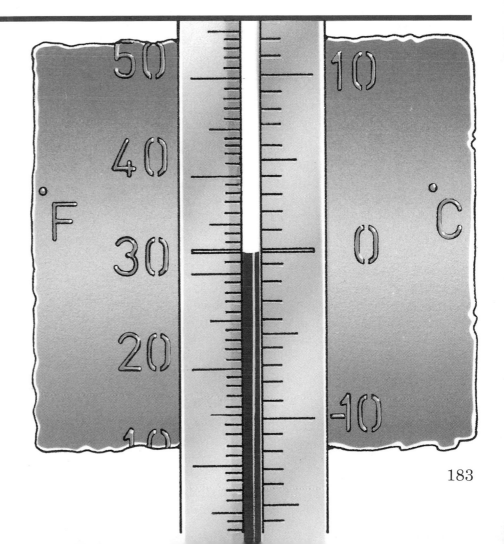

If there are more trees in the mountains than in the city, why is there more oxygen in the city than in the mountains?

Raudy Steele
Westcliffe, Colorado

You are correct that there is less oxygen in the air high in the mountains. But I think the rest of your idea is not quite right.

Cities are usually in valleys so that when you go to the mountains you go up higher. As you go higher, there is less air above you. So, there's less pressure from the air above squeezing on the air around you. A common way to say this is that as you go higher, the air around you gets thinner.

Getting thinner means that a quart of air has less air in it. That's why it has less oxygen.

How did Columbus prove the earth is round?

Karen Raplee
Pine City, New York

The idea that the earth is round seems to have been stated almost 2,000 years before Columbus. However, proving the idea was not as easy as it is today. Proving the idea so that everyone could understand it was even harder. After all, the earth does *seem* to be flat (except for its mountains and valleys). I suppose that at the time of Columbus, when very few people could even read and write, most people believed only what they could see and feel.

Columbus knew the earth had to be round. If that were true, then he could get to China in the east by sailing west. That meant sailing out across the Atlantic Ocean, where no one had ever gone before. And that took a lot of courage, especially since most people (including his sailors) thought he was crazy.

Of course, Columbus did not get all the way round the world, so you could say he didn't completely prove it was round. What he did do was to make it easier for everyone to understand the idea.

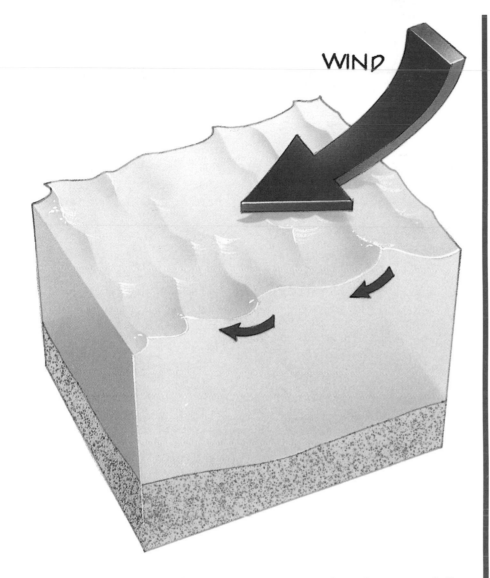

WIND

What makes waves curl as they reach the shore?

*Stacey Canada
Jonesboro, Arkansas*

People have been watching waves for a long time. And books have been written about them. Just as you noticed, something happens to ocean waves as they come to the shallow water near shore. Exactly how this works depends on the shape of the beach.

Let's suppose we are watching very regular ocean waves coming in toward a gradually sloping beach. As the water begins to get shallower, water movement is slowed by friction against the bottom. The waves are slowed down and pushed together. That makes each wave steeper, especially on its front side. As the water gets more shallow, the waves get steeper and steeper until they fall over and break on the front side.

Usually a wave breaks when the water depth is about $1\frac{1}{3}$ times the height of the waves. A lot more is going on inside a wave that we did not talk about. But maybe you can see why waves break as they move into shallow water.

What causes waves?

*Heather MacKay
Kokomo, Indiana*

Most waves that you can see every day are caused by the wind. As air blows across a water surface there is a little friction between the air and water. That tends to slow down the lowest layer of air and drag along some of the upper layer of water. You have noticed that a blowing wind does not blow smoothly. Almost always it is gusty or churning around. So, the drag on the surface is uneven. That's enough to make little waves.

Once there are little waves, the wind pushes against them to make bigger waves. As the wind goes farther and farther across the ocean, the waves get bigger and farther apart.

You can make your own waves. Put a big dinner plate on the kitchen drain board and fill it almost level-full with water. Now get down close and blow across the surface of the surface of the plate. You can see why wind and waves go together.

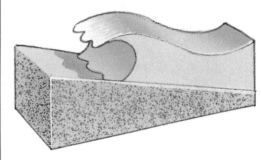

185

When you write with a pencil, how does the lead work?

Jennifer Buttlar
Nashua, New Hampshire

The lead in your pencil is made out of graphite, a form of carbon, with some clay added in. About four hundred years ago when people learned to use graphite for writing, people supposed that it was a form of the element lead. So, the black stuff in the center of a pencil is still called the lead.

A pencil works to make marks on a paper because it is soft enough to rub off on the paper. It's also soft enough to scrape down to a point when you sharpen the pencil.

Where does the Sun go when the Moon comes out? Where does the Moon go when the Sun comes out? Does the Moon make night? Does the Sun make day? I don't know the answers, but I like day more.

Vicki Doucet
Bathurst, New Brunswick

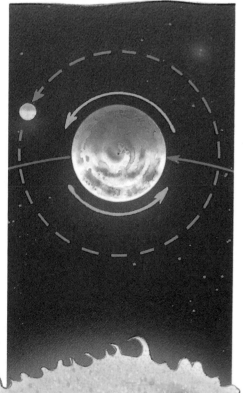

The Sun is a hot glowing ball that gives us light and keeps us warm. Our Earth is revolving around the Sun like a big spinning ball. So, about half the time the Sun seems to be overhead and it is daytime. And about half the time the Sun is on the other side and it is night on our side.

The Moon is always making a big circle around the earth. We see it when it is only on our side of the earth. And we see it only in light that it reflects back to us from the Sun. Sometimes you can see the Moon during the daytime, but then it looks only a little brighter than the sky behind it.

The Moon looks best when we see it at night. Then it looks very bright against the dark sky.

What are diamonds made of?

Kristi Ann Garatti
Thunder Bay, Ontario

Diamonds are made out of the element carbon. So, all the atoms in a diamond are alike. Each one is bonded to four neighboring carbons, each exactly the same distance away. Once they get put together that way, it is very difficult to move them around. So, a diamond is one of the hardest substances we have.

There are other ways to put carbon atoms together. So, we have other substances—like charcoal and lampblack and graphite—also made out of carbon. Chemists like to talk about these different forms of carbon. They show that even when substances are made from just one kind of atom, their properties depend on the way the atoms are hooked together.

What are chemicals made of?

Jason Creppel
Harvey, Louisiana

One answer is that chemicals are made out of molecules, tiny particles way too small to see even with a microscope. There are many different kinds of molecules. Each kind is made out of a particular combination of atoms. An atom is the smallest particle of an element and there are more than 100 different kinds of elements.

What I have just said is true about any substance you can think of—rocks and dirt and wood and even your body. But when you talk about a chemical, you usually think of a pure substance made out of just one kind of molecule.

One chemical you see in almost pure form every day is ordinary table salt. Each one of its molecules is made out of one atom of sodium and one atom of chlorine. So, its name is sodium chloride.

Now you can think like a chemist.

I have chosen the topic windmills for a science fair project. My question is: Are windmills still useful today?

Jamie White
West Bridgewater, Massachusetts

I hope you have learned a lot about windmills. They were invented over a thousand years ago, long before people had any steam or gas engines. A hard job that took a lot of work was the grinding of grain to make a kind of flour. It seems that grinding grain was the common work done by windmills in Europe for several hundred years. They are not used for that anymore because we have much better sources of energy, like electric and gasoline motors.

In the United States windmills came into wide use as a way of pumping water. There aren't so many anymore. It's easier and cheaper to use an electric motor than to repair a windmill. But there are still some working out West, mostly in lonely places without close-by electricity. I think you can still buy those windmills built like big fans and held up on steel towers.

Nowadays we are searching for sources of energy that don't depend on the burning of coal and oil. So, engineers are working with windmills again to see if they can make them good enough to generate electricity practically. Of course, wind (like sunlight) is free. But the trick is to build a windmill that will generate electricity cheaply and reliably.

I guess we have to say that, even though we now have other sources of energy, windmills are still useful.

Suppose you stopped at the stop sign. Is the gas used by the car being wasted?

Mary Haryan
Syracuse, New York

You are exactly right that the gasoline used by an automobile at a stop sign is being wasted. Trouble is, if the stop is only very brief, it is better to use this gas than to restart your car. That may not be true while waiting alongside a curb for a friend. I am glad you are thinking about the way we use gasoline.

What is compost, and what is it used for?

Kelly Stewart
Fairfield, Ohio

Compost can be made out of anything that will rot or decay.

It is commonly made out of grass clippings, leaves, or even garbage. It works in the same way as the recycling processes of nature.

Think of all the leaves that fall from trees every autumn. During the year they slowly just seem to disappear. We say that they decompose or rot or decay. What we mean is that they became food for the molds and bacteria of soil. Only some of their fibers are left to become a part of the soil and decay more slowly.

Composting uses the same idea but usually is done by piling stuff together, maybe in an open box. (Most people don't put meat scraps in compost mainly because decaying meat usually smells bad.) The compost that results is good fertilizer for gardens and lawns.

189

Do rocks grow?

David Dion
Framingham, Massachusetts

Do rocks grow? No, not in the sense that living things grow. Of course, when rocks were formed, or when they are being formed now, they are increasing in size. Think of a stalactite, which looks like a rock icicle hanging from the ceiling of a cave. It increases in size as ground water drips over it and leaves calcium carbonate behind, little by little.

You might say that it grows, but you will see that it really increases in size only by adding more of itself to its outside. Living things do not grow that way. An animal takes in food and changes the food to make more animal.

How do clouds float when there is gravity and feathers can't?

Sarah McMurray
Oxnard, California

I like your question. It shows that you are a good observer and curious about nature. And it isn't easy to see why clouds should be able to stay up when something as light as a feather can't.

A cloud is made out of jillions of tiny water droplets. Each droplet all by itself is too small for your eye to see. Each droplet is pulled toward the earth just like anything else.

But tiny particles have lots more surface compared to their weight. That gives a lot of friction in moving through air. Because of that they fall very slowly.

Even though they fall slowly, something else must work to keep cloud droplets from falling to the ground. What keeps them up there are upward-blowing drafts of air. If you have watched clouds, you have noticed that they are always changing in shape. They are always moving in those gusty winds that hold them up there.

You can see that it takes a lot of different ideas to understand why clouds behave the way they do.

Since there is gravity on both ends of the earth, would it be true that if someone dug a hole through the earth he could stay in the middle without falling through?

Jill Schmidt
Wichita, Kansas

I asked my friend Claude Horton to help answer your question. Here is his answer.

"We are used to thinking of falling toward the earth. What we call gravity is the attraction between the very great mass of the earth and the mass of another object, like your body.

"In talking about the gravitational force between two objects, we can treat each object as if its mass were concentrated at its very center.

"When we get inside the earth, as in a deep mine shaft, things get more complicated. Then an object is closer to the center of the earth, and we would expect the gravitational force toward the center to be even greater. But there is also some mass of earth nearer the surface that causes an upward force on the object. The result of these two attractions is a force toward the center of the earth, but it is smaller than the force at the surface.

"The easiest way to answer your question is to think about ideal conditions. This is a trick that physicists often use to make things as simple as possible. We will imagine that there is no friction, that your body never scrapes against the side of the hole, and that there is no air to slow down its motion. Then if you fell in, you would fall all the way through and come to the surface at the other end of the hole.

"Of course, you would fall right back again. If no one stopped your motion, you would oscillate forever, falling back and forth from one end of the hole to the other.

"If there is even a small amount of friction with air or by rubbing against the sides of the hole, the answer will be different. Then if you fell into the hole, you would never quite reach the other side. You would oscillate back and forth; but each travel would be shorter than the one before—like a swing dying down. In time you would come to rest right at the center of the earth.

"I am sure you understand that we have talked about a completely imaginary problem and not any real experiment. The center of the earth has a very hot liquid core, and no one thinks seriously of drilling a hole through it. And even if we could do such an experiment, I do not think you would want to fall in just to see if I am right."

Once I went to Yellowstone and saw geysers. I would like to know more about them.

Chris Haley
Cincinnati, Ohio

I am glad you got to see the Yellowstone geysers. As I remember, the Park Service there has a display showing how geysers work. The next time you are there, ask a park ranger to show you the geyser display.

There is a simple way to tell the idea of how a geyser works. It's something like a coffee percolator. There has to be a hot place down deep in the ground and some way for water to get down to it.

Geysers occur only where the hot molten interior of the earth comes close enough to the surface. That heats up the rocks down below. Water falling on the hot rock gets turned into steam, which expands with great force. That drives out steam and hot water. If there is a hole to the surface above and a cave that can hold part of the water running down, that gives the special formation needed to make a geyser.

I have not told you all about geysers, but maybe enough so you can see the idea of how they work.

Why doesn't a rubber band shoot underwater, and why doesn't a bubble sink in water?

Norman Kuong
Chicago, Illinois

A rubber band does not "shoot" very well underwater. This is because the water is thicker (denser) than air, so the water puts up more resistance. It's easy to notice that it is harder to push your hand through water than it is to wave your hand through the air.

A bubble of air is a lot lighter than the same volume of water. When a bubble is formed underwater, the much heavier water tries to take its place, and that pushes the bubble to the surface.

You may wonder why some bars of soap float on water and others sink. The companies that make their soap to float trap air inside the soap bar. That carries the soap to the top of the water.

I would like to know why water foams, like in a river when the water goes over a fall.

Laura Ernst
Stoughton, Massachusetts

I think foam is made by churning up water and getting some air bubbles in it. In very pure water the bubbles break very quickly. However, it is difficult to get very pure water, even in a chemistry laboratory. The difficulty is that so many things dissolve in water. Even in a mountain stream the water contains substances from rocks and soil and fish that help to make bubbles and some foam.

Of course, you know that some things, like soap, help to make water foam. So, streams that contain soaplike stuff are likely to be foamier. I think that if you could make a small river from the water of your bathtub it would be pretty foamy.

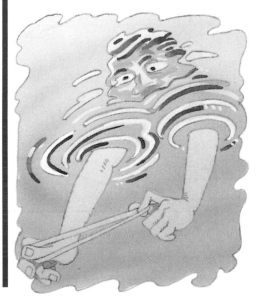

193

Once when I looked into a spoon, I was upside down. Can you explain why this is so?

Shan Scott
Oxon Hill, Maryland

The shiny surface of a spoon makes a good mirror for bouncing back, or reflecting, light rays. And the inside of a spoon has a cupped-in surface so that it is called a **concave** mirror. If you are far enough away from it, any concave mirror behaves just the way you described.

One common way to show how mirrors work is to use lines to describe the path of light rays and make a scale diagram. I will make such a diagram and will tell you what it means.

First I drew a part of a circle to represent the curved surface of the mirror. Then I drew the arrow AB to represent an *object*. I used an arrow only because it is easier to draw than a man. Then I drew in four light rays. The *a* lines start from A, the tip of the arrow, and the *b* lines start from B, the back end of the arrow. The upper *a* line strikes the mirror at an angle and is reflected back at an angle. The lower *a* line strikes the mirror head on and is reflected straight back. If you draw them correctly, all possible rays of light from A to the mirror will be reflected so that they pass through point A'. I drew only two of them to show the idea. Also, all possible rays of light from point B, like the *b* lines shown, will past through point B'.

An object like the arrow AB really is described by a large number of points, and we could draw more lines to show rays from many more of them. But just the lines from A and B are enough to show the idea: the convex mirror will form an image A'B' of the object AB.

In looking into a spoon, you are the object like the arrow AB, and you see yourself reflected like the image A'B'. Notice two things about the image in the diagram. First, it is smaller than the object. Secondly, it is inverted, or upside down. The image of yourself that you see in a spoon works the same way.

You might also notice how your image changes when you hold the spoon up and down or crosswise. One way you will look tall and skinny, the other way short and fat. Maybe you have already guessed why. The spoon has one curvature along it, and a different curvature across it. The inside of a spoon is really a very complex kind of concave mirror.

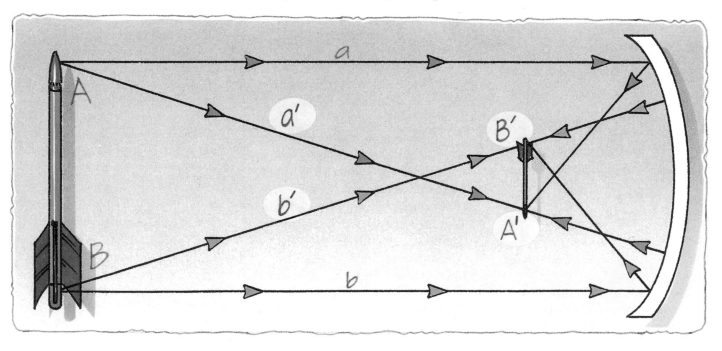

When a car is traveling forward, why do the wheels appear to be rotating backward?

Ben Leary
Donelson, Tennessee

That doesn't happen when you are looking directly at a real car. But it does occur sometimes when you see a car in the movies or on TV.

The effect occurs for the same reason in moving pictures and on TV: We are looking at a series of picture taken in rapid succession. Our eyes smear the successive pictures together so that we think we are seeing smooth and continuous motion. This works fine until we start to look at rapid repetitive motions like the spokes of a turning wheel.

The effect is easier for me to think about in movies because then we have completely separate pictures taken at a rate of 24 per second and projected at the same speed. Let's describe the position of one spoke of a wheel as if it were the hour hand of a clock. Let's suppose the wheel is turning clockwise and at a special speed. Suppose that in 1/24th of a second (the time between pictures) one spoke of the wheel doesn't make a full turn. Suppose that in one picture it is straight up at the 12 o'clock position, and in the next picture it has turned only to the 11 o'clock position. And so on. You can see that even if the wheel is turning forward (clockwise), it will seem to be turning backward.

TV gives the effect for just the same basic reason, although pictures on a TV screen are more complex and they come at a different rate, I believe 30 pictures per second.

195

Why does cabbage grow above ground and a carrot grow under the ground?

Ann Jacobe
Island Lake, Illinois

Of course, you know that both have parts both places. Almost all garden plants have the same kinds of parts. They have roots and stems and leaves. And most of them make seeds. Some kinds of plants, like lettuce and cabbage, make leaves that are good to eat. Some, like carrots and turnips, make big fleshy roots that are good. And some, like wheat and corn and rice, make seeds that we eat.

Out of all the very many kinds of plants on earth we have picked a few to grow because they have a part that is good to eat. There is no law that says you can't eat a corn root or a carrot leaf if you want to. But these are not likely to be very good food, and I doubt that you will ever find them in supermarkets.

My brother and I found some seashell fossils. We can't explain why there are those type fossils in this area because our area is very hilly. We don't know if the ocean came up to here or not. Can you explain it?

Patrick Walker
Waco, Texas

I think it is not really any great surprise to find seashell fossils near Waco where you live. There are also many of them where I live near Austin.

Of course, it does seem a surprise at first because this part of the country is hilly and a long way from the seacoast. The face of our earth has changed a lot in its long, long history. Finding fossils of marine animals shows you that this part of the earth must have been under the ocean when those animals were alive millions of years ago.

NORTH AMERICA: 75 MILLION YEARS AGO

Has anyone ever tried to make oil? If they could figure out how the decaying material was changed into oil, couldn't they just use a similar process but speed it up?

Anna Shoeman
Biddeford, Maine

I think that's a good question and a good idea. It is so good that there must be some reason why we are not doing that right now.

One problem is that we do not know exactly how oil (petroleum) was made. The most common idea is that it was made from the fats and oils of algae (or plankton). There is not any big mass of algae grown anywhere in any one year. But our oil, some of it deep within the ground, could have been made very slowly. It seems to have been made and stored up over more than a hundred million years. We are using up the oil much faster than it could have been made. So that's the second problem: if we made oil from algae growing in nature, we could not make it fast enough.

You might like to know that some scientists at the Solar Energy Research Institute in Golden, Colorado, are working on an idea like yours. They are trying to see if we could grow algae a lot faster than algae grow in nature and maybe find special kinds that makes lots of fats and oils. The idea is to change solar energy into the stored-up energy in vegetable oil. That isn't quite the same as petroleum that we get out of the ground, but it does have lots of energy. There is no doubt that we can do this. The question is how much that kind of oil would cost.

I really don't think your idea would work. But you should not be discouraged. I have had lots of bright ideas that never worked.

Why does lightning prefer to hit high places rather than low?

Rheanna Doncses
Valrico, Florida

Lightning occurs as a discharge of electricity. Usually there has been a big accumulation of negative charge at the lower levels of a cloud. The discharge is like a big spark going through the air toward the ground. Air is not very good at conducting electricity. Almost anything that sticks up high makes a better pathway. So, anything that sticks up high is more likely to get hit by lightning.

Lightning will often hit a tall tree. A tall metal building, like the Empire State Building, is still better. Like water running downhill, a negative electric charge seeking a positive charge will take the easiest path.

Some people say that there are no living things on the Moon, but I think that the astronauts put living things on the Moon. Do you think so?

Sylvia Huang
New Rochelle, New York

I think you are right that the astronauts, even though they tried to be very clean, must have left some bacteria on the surface of the Moon. That happened in the early 1970s.

One reason to suppose that there is no life on the Moon is that it's not a very friendly place for life. Temperatures change from way below zero at night to more than 100° Celsius in full sunlight. There isn't any water, and there's no air. So it's likely that any bacteria the astronauts took to the Moon have long since died out.

I think we can safely say that there is probably no life on the Moon.

What are cosmic rays?

*Jeff Nichols
Davenport, Iowa*

When scientists were first learning about radioactive elements, they invented instruments for detecting the radiation coming off. One of these is called a Geiger counter. It counts, usually with clicks you can hear, ionizations in air produced by X rays and high-speed particles.

When a Geiger counter is brought close to radioactive material, like radium or uranium, it clicks away rapidly and tells about how much radiation is there. But there was a surprise that no matter where they were, Geiger counters always slowly clicked away. They clicked still more slowly with shields of lead around them or when placed in mines deep in the earth. Finally, it turned out that some radiation is coming to us from outer space. That is called cosmic rays.

Study has shown that cosmic rays are high-speed particles, the nuclei of atoms. They seem to come from outside the solar system, maybe from exploding stars.

More cosmic rays are detected at high altitude, so the blanket of our air screens out most of them and not many are left at ground level. Someone has estimated that the energy in cosmic rays is about the same as starlight. I suspect that the astronauts in walking on the Moon received more cosmic rays than you will in your lifetime. So, you should not worry about them. I don't.

199

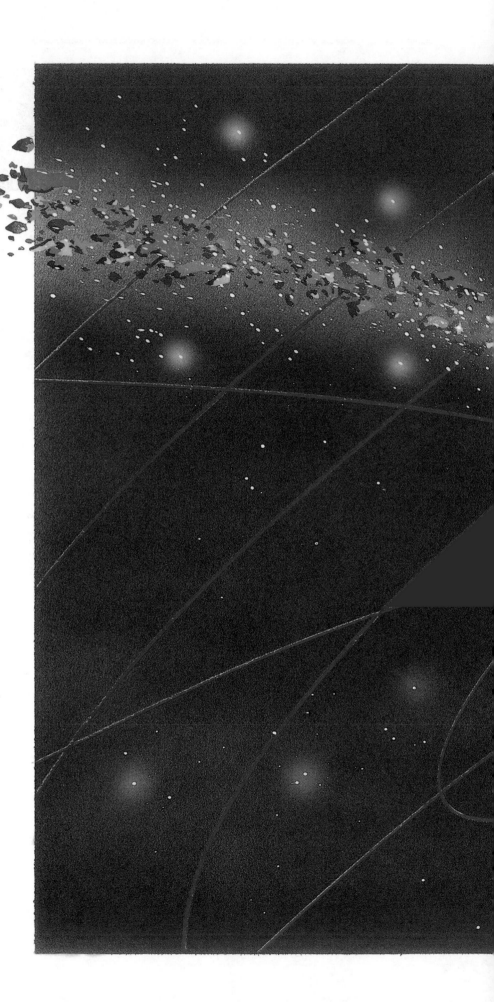

What happens to stuff that falls into a black hole?

Patrick Walker
Waco, Texas

I do not know much about black holes except the idea of how they are formed.

At some time in its very long life, a star may use up the nuclear energy that keeps it in the form of a hot gas. Then it contracts and gets smaller. It may become a dwarf star with all its matter squeezed more tightly together. However, if it was very large to start with, it will have a very great mass and pull of gravity. The idea is that maybe the force pulling all that stuff together can get so great that it crushes itself down to almost nothing at all.

A black hole is a place where not even light can escape. That's why it's called a black hole. So I guess that anything that fell in would get crushed down to almost nothing at all.

Why can't you see the wind?

Shannon Clonch
Reynoldsburg, Ohio

I wondered why you would ask that question. Maybe it is because you can *feel* the wind. So why can't you see it?

The answer is so simple that it isn't much fun. You can't see the air around you. And wind is only moving air. So you can't see the wind, either.

Maybe you would like to turn the question around. If we can't see the air, how do we know it's there? Because we can feel it when it moves as wind. If there were no air, planes and birds couldn't fly— and you couldn't breathe.

Where does the wind come from?

Ben Bowen
Orlando, Florida

You know that the earth is kept warm by sunlight. But the earth is not warmed evenly over all of its surface. At any one time about half is in sunlight during the day and the other half is in the shade which we call night. And since the earth is an almost-round ball, there will always be some part (near the equator) on which sunlight hits head on and other parts (near the poles) where sunlight hits at an angle.

Above any warm spot on the earth's surface, the air is heated. Warm air expands to become lighter, and it rises. So there are always some places where air is expanding and rising and some places where air is cooling and moving downward.

This uneven heating and cooling is enough to start air in motion to make wind. Then a lot of other things happen. Air moving over the ocean picks up lots of water vapor. Then if that air gets cooled, it forms clouds. So the air above us is always churning around to give us all the changes that the weatherman talks about.

What makes popcorn pop?

Kimberly Gail Anderson
Alma, Arkansas

Popcorn is a special kind of corn. One thing that makes it special is that each grain has a thin, but very tight coat. When you heat it up, the little bit of water inside turns to steam. Because the steam can't get out through the coat, the whole grain of corn explodes.

Good popping popcorn must have just the right moisture content so there will be just the right amount of steam in the grains and all of them will pop.

Happy popping. I like it, too.

Since salt is not hot, how does it melt ice and snow?

Michael Gray
Guelph, Ontario

The freezing point of water, the temperature just cold enough to make it freeze into ice, is 0 degrees Celsius. Dissolving salt in water makes the water harder to freeze. To get salt water to freeze you have to make it colder than 0 degrees. So you can say that salt lowers the freezing point of water.

If you add salt to ice, some of the salt will melt. You can suppose that the salt pulls some water away from its crystal form in ice. When that happens the ice-salt mixture will get colder than 0 degrees.

Here is a recipe for making a very cold freezing mixture: Mix 33 ounces of salt with 100 ounces of snow or finely crushed ice. That is supposed to give a temperature of minus 21 degrees C.

When you put dry ice and warm water together, why does smoke pour out of the container? And why does dry ice put out fire?

Abby Hosford
Gainesville, Georgia

Dry ice is interesting stuff. It is frozen carbon dioxide. Its temperature is about minus 79 degrees Celsius. When it is warmed, instead of turning into a liquid, it turns right into a gas. A single teaspoon of dry ice will make several quarts of pure carbon dioxide gas.

Now we can think about the answers to your questions. When you drop a piece of dry ice into warm water, it rapidly turns into gas and bubbles out. As it does, it carries some water vapor out into the air. Then some of the water vapor condenses into droplets and appears as steam.

Carbon dioxide is good for putting out fires if it surrounds the fire and keeps oxygen away. So liquid carbon dioxide is held under pressure in some fire extinguishers and kept just for use on a fire. Since carbon dioxide is a heavy gas—heavier than air—it works best on a fire in a low place.

Dry ice is fun, but also dangerous. You should never try to pick it up with your fingers. It will cause frostbite just as bad as a burn.

If heat makes things expand and cold makes them contract, why does water expand when you freeze it?

Jenny Tudesko
Sacramento, California

Water is very common. But in some ways it is also very strange and different than anything else we know.

Water is strangest when it is a liquid, as we usually see it. Because its molecules are so sticky to each other, they find ways to snuggle in tightly to each other and still move around.

When water freezes, its molecules lock themselves into a special pattern of six-sided figures. In that pattern the molecules take up more room than they did in the liquid. So water expands as it freezes from liquid water into crystals of ice.

Why does ice last longer on a hot day if you wrap it in something?

Nathan Bennett
Tulsa, Oklahoma

Let's think about the problem this way. Ice melts because heat flows to it from something else. The heat makes the ice melt. And something else that gave up the heat gets colder.

Some materials carry heat very readily and we say that they are good conductors. Most metals, especially copper, are good conductors. Other materials do not carry heat very well and we call them insulators. To keep ice from melting we want to surround it with an insulator.

Just wrapping newspapers around a piece of ice slows the melting. The newspaper is a pretty good insulator, at least until it gets soppy wet.

Why do the sun and moon seem to follow me when I'm riding in a car?

Joshua Woehrer
Milwaukee, Wisconsin

I think everyone has had that feeling. When you are traveling in a car, buildings, fences, and signs go by you in a hurry but the sun or moon just seem to hang up there as if they were following you. This happens because the sun and the moon are so very far away—thousands of times farther than anything you can see on earth.

The farther away something is the more slowly it seems to move. Here's a simple way to see that. Watch a bird swoosh by as it flies across your yard. Then watch a jet plane high in the sky. The plane may be flying at almost four hundred miles an hour, but it seems to move very slowly because it is several miles away. The bird is flying only about a tenth as fast as a jet plane but it goes by in a hurry because it is so much closer.

Our eyes give us pictures of the world around us. But our eyes don't tell us enough about how far away things are. That part we have to get used to.

When electricity makes things hot, does the electricity get hot?

Jenny Stoops
Brownsburg, Indiana

Electricity is a form of energy, not an object that takes up space. When electricity passes through anything, even a copper wire, some of it is lost and appears in another form of energy which we call heat. You can use electricity to heat an electric iron. Some of the electricity is used up to make heat so that the iron gets hot.

You can say the same thing about light. Think of a sidewalk on a sunny day. Sunlight falling upon it is absorbed and changed into heat. So the sidewalk gets warmer.

You may think this is all a little bit tricky. We can say that electricity can be changed into heat. But we do not say that electricity gets hot.

How are tapes made for a tape recorder?

Michael Zions
Far Rockaway, New York

We can transfer the sounds of your voice into changes in an electric current, and then transfer the changes of electric current back into sound. That's what a telephone does. That's how a tape recorder works, too.

What a tape must do is to "remember" the changes in electric current so we can play them back and listen to them later.

The tape remembers with its thousands of tiny magnetic particles. The recording head is an electromagnet. As the tape passes over the head, a changing electric current arranges the magnetic particles in a special pattern. Then, when you pull the tape back across the head, you set up the same special pattern of electric current which can be turned back into sound.

Of course, we can also record much more complicated things—like a whole movie. But the idea is always the same.

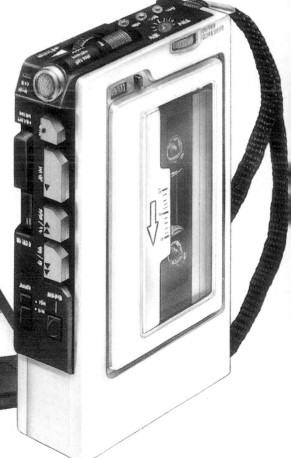

207

When I asked my dad why an apple turns brown when you take a bite out of it or why a banana turns brown when you peel it, he said it had something to do with oxygen and the fruit. Could you explain?

Jane Bradshaw
Rockport, Texas

You dad is correct. The darkening actually needs three different things: oxygen, tyrosine, and an enzyme called tyrosinase. You know about oxygen. Tyrosine is an amino acid, one of the things used to build protein. Some of it is present in almost all living tissues.

Tyrosinase is an enzyme. That means it has the power to speed up some special chemical reaction. By themselves, oxygen and tyrosine react so slowly that you would get tired watching them to see anything happen. But if just a few molecules of tyrosinase are around, there is a rapid chemical reaction. Oxygen combines with tyrosine molecules and ties them together to make a dark stuff called melanin. That's why a cut apple darkens. And the same thing happens to a cut banana or potato.

You might be interested to know that melanin is a very common dark pigment formed also in the skin or hairs or feathers of animals.

Some friends who are good cooks tell me that there is an easy way to keep apples from darkening when you cut them up for a salad. Sprinkle on a little lemon juice. That contains ascorbic acid (also called vitamin C), which prevents the oxidation of tyrosine. Why don't you try this and see if the lemon juice will slow down the darkening of a cut apple?

How does a plant grow by just planting it in the mud?

Benjamin Orgeron
Harvey, Louisiana

I never thought of plants as being unusual, but when you say it that way maybe they are.

I suppose you are thinking about planting a seed. That's really a baby or embryo plant with some stored food material around it, carefully protected by a tough coat. It will stay that way, sometimes for years as long as it is kept dry.

The seed changes when it gets warm and moist. Then it starts to grow and bursts out of the tough coat. It makes a root that grows downward and a stem that grows upward.

All this depends on the food material stored in the seed, which lasts until the little plant has made some green leaves. Then it can use sunlight to make its own food.

So, for a plant, warm mud is really a good place to begin life.

Why do pine trees keep their leaves in winter?

Ivan Middleton
Adrian, Michigan

You probably have noticed that the trees which keep their leaves through the winter—like the pines, spruces, and firs—have special leaves that are like tough little needles. These have a lot less water than the thin, flat leaves that fall from other trees in autumn.

Those needlelike leaves of the pine tree also have a special ability to stand below-freezing temperatures without damage. Most organisms that can do that have some special "antifreeze" chemicals.

Scientists are learning more about these. The big danger of freezing is the formation of ice crystals which push right through cell membranes and kill the tissue. Some of the "antifreeze" chemicals work to prevent the formation of ice crystals. I think that's a neat trick.

I pushed my finger into a soap bubble, but it didn't pop. Why not?

Patricia West
Birmingham, Alabama

Soap bubbles are surprising in the way they behave. And there are many interesting things you can do with them.

Soap bubbles pop when the film of soap and water around them gets stretched too thin or if the water in the film evaporates. If you were in a bathtub your fingers probably were wet and soapy. Touching a soap bubble with a dry object is more likely to break it.

Why do you need two holes to pour juice out of a can?

Philomena Zito
Pomona, New Jersey

This happens because the pressure of air around us pushes inward against the hole. This actually is much greater than the pressure of the juice trying to get out. You would need a juice can about thirty-two feet tall to give the juice at the hole enough pressure to force itself out against the air pressure.

When you make a second hole you give air a way to get in and bubble up inside the can. Then air pressure is working about equally both inside and outside the can. And the pressure of the juice makes it run out of the lowest hole.

Maybe another way to say all this is that you need two holes, one to let the juice out and one to let air in. Of course, just one big hole also will work because it can let air bubble in and juice come out, too.

I was drinking a can of soda through a straw. I put my index finger on top of the straw and lifted it up. The soda would not pour out of the straw until I lifted my finger. Why?

Roslyn Davis
East Hartford, Connecticut

The soda is held up and can't leave unless air can get in to take its place. Your finger on top of the straw seals it off against air pressure from that direction. But air pressure pushing upward is just as great as the weight of the water pushing downward. When you take your finger away, air pressure pushes equally on the top and bottom of the straw. Then the soda's weight makes it run out.

Chemists use that same trick to measure and transfer solutions. They use glass tubes called pipettes.

How come when you drop something into a bottle of soda, bubbles come up and make the soda spill all over the place?

Chris Coleman
Montgomery, Alabama

Soda water is made by dissolving carbon dioxide gas in water or in a flavored solution. This is done under pressure and then the bottle is capped.

When you take off the cap and release the pressure, carbon dioxide wants to come out of the solution and make bubbles. Unless the bottle is warmed or shaken, this usually will happen slowly. The soda water will keep its soda (carbon dioxide) long enough to taste good while you drink it.

Most things that you might drop into the bottle, especially if they have rough surfaces or sharp edges, help the carbon dioxide come out of the solution and form bubbles faster.

211

Why does aging wood on a house turn black?

Sarah Adams
Griffin, Georgia

Since I did not have an answer to your question, I wrote to the Forest Products Laboratory in Madison, Wisconsin. The scientists there know nearly all there is to know about wood. They sent me a bulletin that contains an answer to your question.

When exposed to the weather, dark-colored woods may become lighter but light-colored woods usually become darker. In time almost any wood ends up as black or some shade of gray and its surface becomes rough. Wood is made mostly of fibers of cellulose, the same stuff that makes up cotton. Wood is hard because the cellulose fibers are cemented together by another stuff called lignin. The lignin and the colored substances in wood are slowly broken down by light and washed out by rain. That gives the wood a rough surface and tends to make it lighter in color. But while all this is going on, micro-organisms, like fungi, may grow on the wood and add their dark colors to make it gray and blotchy or sometimes even black.

You can see why we usually coat wood with a paint or stain to protect it against the weather and prevent all these changes from happening.

Why does dust seem to move along a beam of sunlight in the same direction as the light?

Tiffany Sharp
Kansas City, Missouri

I have watched dust particles in a beam of sunlight in the way you suggest. Sometimes it does seem as if dust particles are moving in the direction of the light beam. However, I think that is likely to be just an accident, or maybe our eyes fool us.

Light does exert a very small pressure, but this is so small that there is no simple way to show it. Particles in the air are moved about mainly by small air currents. The push of light on a dust particle is much smaller than the push of even very small air movements.

What is house dust?

Diana Hedgpeth
Torrance, California

House dust has lots of things in it and just what it contains probably differs in different houses. Because it has such fine particles, you would need a microscope to see what is there. As in most dust, it is likely to have tiny particles of soil or sand, pollen dust from flowers, and spores produced by micro-organisms such as molds. It is also likely to have little fibers of lint from rugs and clothing and hair. Some people get asthma or allergies like hay fever from house dust.

213

How come when I am out in the sun my skin gets darker but my shirt fades?

Kelly Holt
Willsboro, New York

You've made an interesting observation. There are many photochemical reactions—chemical reactions brought about by light. Many colored materials absorb light and help bring about photochemical reactions which change them and destroy their color. That happens to many dyes used to color our clothes.

Sunlight, especially the ultraviolet part of it, is bad for living cells because it causes many destructive photochemical reactions. One of these gives you sunburn. Your skin tries to help protect you by making a dark pigment called melanin. Melanin acts as a screen in absorbing light close to the surface of your skin. Dark skin already has a lot of melanin. And some people form melanin and get tanned more easily than others. However, overexposure to sunlight is not good for anyone.

Are black and white colors?

Jaime Foster
Rock Island, Illinois

I think you might get either a yes or a no answer on this, depending on what someone is thinking about when answering the question.

If you are a printer with different color inks, black ink would be one of them. And of the different papers you might choose, one would be white.

But I would say no, they are not colors. Something white, like snow or white paper, is white because it reflects light of all colors equally. And something black, like coal, is black because it absorbs light of all colors equally. Something that is colored, like a rose, will be red if it reflects red light and absorbs light of other colors.

You can see why I think the answer is no. But I would not like to argue about this question with a printer.

Why does black absorb heat better than other colors?

Sumana Reddy
Norcross, Georgia

Black is black because it absorbs all colors of light. And absorbed light is turned into heat. So if you want something to warm up in sunlight, paint it black.

Now I can ask you. What color would you paint an object which you want to stay as cool as possible in sunlight?

215

When you hit or touch something, why does it make a sound?

Sara Clark
Owaneco, Illinois

If you hit your desktop with a pencil you set up some vibrations, some in the desktop and some in the pencil. These vibrations set up vibrations in air that are carried in the air to your ears. Your ear can hear vibrations like that. We call them sound.

How does that sound to you?

How come if you go into the bathroom to sing it sounds better than when you are in the bedroom or anywhere else?

Glonar Fonseca
Lemoore, California

I congratulate you on having a good singing voice. I used to try singing in the bathroom and it sounded great to me. But my family never thought it was much of an improvement.

I think bathroom singing is special and may make your voice sound better. Bathrooms, especially around tubs and shower stalls, have bare walls that make nice crisp echoes and reverberations. That gives your voice extra quality.

One day I was looking at stained glass and I wondered, "How do they stain it?"

Courtney Bennett
Newtown, Pennsylvania

Glass is made by heating compounds of silicon until they melt or fuse. When the hot liquid cools down, it forms glass. Sand (mostly silicon dioxide) can be used by itself, but it needs a very high temperature to be melted. With the addition of some other chemicals, glass can be made at a lower temperature. Sodium carbonate is added to make most window glass, lead oxide to make most crystal, and sodium borate to make Pyrex.

People have been making glass for over a thousand years. At some time along the way they learned that other kinds of minerals melted in with glass would give it special colors. Ruby glass contains copper, blue glass contains cobalt, and green glass usually contains iron. That's what we call stained glass.

Some of the famous stained-glass windows of cathedrals in Europe were made about six hundred years ago. No one knew much about chemistry then, but they found out, just by testing, what minerals to add to get different colors.

I think it is interesting that people learned to make glass and even some of the world's most beautiful stained glass before they knew much of anything about its chemistry.

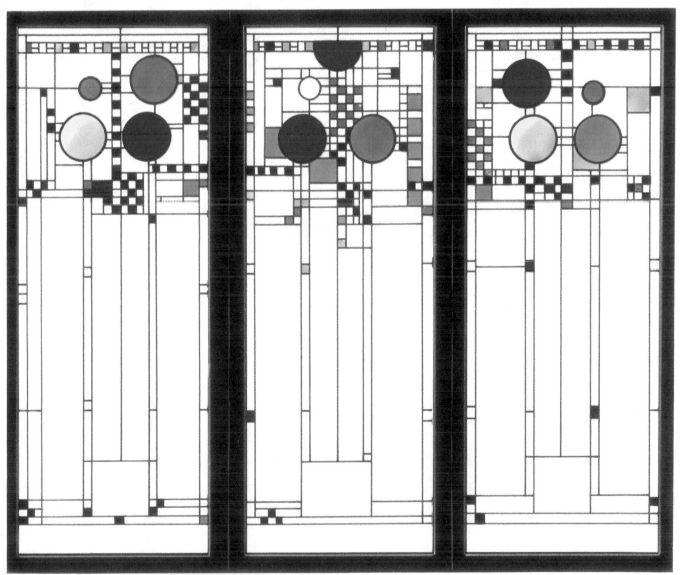

Why does ice stick to cotton?

Tienda Greene
Pikesville, Maryland

It's easy to make ice stick to cotton, but something special must happen. There must be a little water to wet the cotton. This may come from the surface of an ice cube where it is melted just a little by warmer air. And the ice cube, maybe right out of the freezer, must be at a temperature below freezing.

If both those things happen, then the ice cube freezes the water that wets the cotton. So the cotton sticks because it is frozen right to the ice cube.

Why do ice cubes float?

Michael Sciortino
Homer, New York

The fact that ice cubes float on water tells us something important about water. When water freezes and changes into a solid, its molecules arrange themselves so that they occupy more space.

Another way to think about it is that a quart of ice weighs less than a quart of water. The ice is lighter, so it floats.

Most liquid substances contract and occupy less space when they change to their solid forms. For example, a piece of solid lead sinks if dropped into a pot of hot melted lead.

How come you can't see water evaporating?

Sharon Vig
London, Ontario

When water evaporates, water molecules are leaving the surface of the liquid water and going out into the air as a gas which we call water vapor. Water vapor is a colorless gas, so you can't see it in the air. And each molecule is so very tiny that it would take about a million billion billion to fill a tablespoon. So you can't see any effect on the water surface as they leave one by one.

I never thought about it like this before, but I guess you could say that evaporation of water is pretty sneaky.

Why does water ripple when you throw a rock into it?

Danny Anisfeld
Westlake Village, California

I guess we all have chucked rocks into a lake or pond just to watch the ripple or wave they make. On a quiet surface there is a neat circle of a wave that travels outward, getting to be a bigger and bigger circle. You want to know how it gets started.

I think the best way to answer that is to drop a small rock in a pool of water that you can get up close to and see what happens.

I used a big kitchen sink. I wish it had been bigger. I let the surface get quiet and then dropped in a small stone. When you do this, you will need to watch carefully because everything happens quickly.

Here is what I think happens. As the stone goes through the surface it pushes water out of the way and makes a ring of water that bulges above the surface. Then, as the stone passes, water from the bulge rushes in to where the stone had been. I was surprised to see a little fountain of water come back up where the stone had been. All that was followed quickly by the ring of a little wave. I think it was the little fountain that started the wave but I could not be sure.

Why don't you try this? Maybe your eyes will be better than mine at seeing what really happens.

219

I know that rubber balls bounce because, as the ball hits the ground, the rubber dents and springs back, pushing the ball into the air. But why do hard things like marbles bounce?

David Johnson
Williamson, West Virginia

The bounciness of something depends on what we call its elasticity. Elastic materials are those that can be squeezed or bent or dented or stretched and then return to the size or shape they had before. Some materials, like butter, seem to have no elasticity at all.

Most of us think of rubber as being elastic. We can stretch a rubber band or bounce a rubber ball. Of course, air is elastic, too. If we squeeze or compress air it tries to expand again. So air pumped into a rubber cover makes a good bouncy basketball.

Now what about hard things like glass and steel? They are elastic, too. Think about the steel wire used to make the "strings" of a piano. When tapped, they vibrate to make a musical sound. A piano is tuned by stretching each string so that it vibrates at the right pitch. Piano wire is elastic. It is also very hard. One of the common ways to use the elasticity of steel is in springs made by coiling up wire.

Steel ball bearings are very bouncy when they hit together. Each ball is dented, ever so little, but bounces back to its round shape. Glass marbles are hard and elastic in the same way. Hard glass and steel are much more elastic than softer materials like wood or aluminum.

Why are some solid materials hard and elastic and others soft and more buttery? This seems to depend on how tightly the molecules of the substances hold to each other. Suppose the molecules of a substance stick together very tightly. Then it is difficult to push them out of their positions, and the substance is hard. If the molecules do get pushed out of position, they tend to snap back, so the substance is also elastic.

If this explanation is right, then what should we think about rubber? It is soft, but also elastic. We think this is because of the special shape of its molecules. Each rubber molecule is long and kinky and maybe looped around its neighbor. So rubber is elastic because each of its molecules is stretchy. Rubber is a special and unusual substance, soft and easy to stretch but also elastic.

How come people use air to blow out small fires, but also use it to make large fires bigger?

Elise Morrison
Hobbs, New Mexico

I have noticed that, too. And at first it does seem to be a surprise. Air does two opposite things to a fire. It provides oxygen that is needed for anything to burn. If you keep air from getting to a fire, you can put it out.

Air also can cool down a fire. The flame and heat of a fire come from burning gases. A blast of air hard enough to keep the flame away from the fuel will put out a fire.

I guess this is another case of "a little is great, but too much is bad."

When my dad strikes a match, a flame appears. Why?

Lillie Wade
Alexandria, Virginia

A match is a special kind of invention for making fire. The idea is the same as the old trick of twirling a stick round and round while pressing its end into a rounded-out spot in another piece of wood. The friction makes the end of the stick get hot. If some easy-to-burn stuff like wood shavings is right there, it could get hot enough to begin burning.

The head of a match usually has a chemical, like potassium chlorate, and some charcoal or sulfur. The striking surface may have some red phosphorus and fine sand. The idea is to get heat by friction and have something there that is very easy to burn. That's a lot easier than the stick trick.

221

One cold winter night I was sitting by the radiator when I wondered what kept hot air running through it.

Tracy Thomas
Horseheads, New York

There are two kinds of radiators commonly used in houses. One kind has an open grill in the floor or wall with big pipes that bring up hot air from a furnace that is usually in the basement. The hot air may be pushed up by a fan inside. Or sometimes just one or two extra-large pipes from the furnace carry air upward. Warm air is lighter (or less dense) so it tends to rise all by itself.

There is also another kind of radiator that sits in a room and is connected to the furnace by water pipes. Hot water comes up from a furnace below and slowly circulates upward through the radiator and back again. This may have a pump, but usually the water moves because hot water is lighter and tends to rise to the radiator. Then it gets cooler in the radiator and sinks back in another pipe toward the furnace.

So we can use the trick that warmer air or water is lighter to carry heat from a furnace to all the rooms of a house.

If heat rises, why is it cold on top of mountains?

Maggie Ehrgott
Marshall, Washington

You are right that warm air rises. The main place air is heated is at the earth's surface, where it is warmed by sunlight. So there are always updrafts of rising hot air above us.

As we go up in the atmosphere, air pressure continually becomes less. That means the rising air is expanding. And a characteristic of any gas is that it is cooled by expansion. So the draft of warm air that starts rising from the earth's surface continually cools itself as it rises. The temperature goes down three or four degrees Fahrenheit for every thousand feet higher we go.

How does a fan cool a room? I thought moving particles made heat.

Jim Vere
Flemington, New Jersey

You are right that stirring or mixing up any fluid, whether water or air, always warms it a little. A small desk fan makes about as much heat as a 100-watt light bulb. However, by moving the air other things happen, too.

Sometimes we use fans to pull in outside air that may be cooler than the air inside. But even in a closed room, moving air will help keep us cool. Moving air helps to evaporate sweat from your skin more rapidly. That's an important way our body has to try to keep cool on a hot day.

So the idea is that, even though a fan makes a little heat, it also does other things that help to make you feel cool.

On really hot days, most of the kids in my class fan ourselves with notebooks. Our teacher says fanning yourself just makes you hotter. Why?

Deborah Rosen
Albany, New York

You may often see people fanning themselves on a hot day when they must sit somewhere that has no air movement. They certainly must think that fanning makes them feel cooler. However, I can see how the answer to your question could go either way.

Moving air cools your skin by evaporating a little sweat. That may happen even when you can't see any sweat at all. In fact, the main use of sweat by your body is to try to keep it cool. And that works better in moving air than in quiet air.

But there is also another part of the problem. It takes energy to move air. Fanning yourself means that some of the muscles in your hand and arm are working. Whenever your muscles work, they also make extra heat. That tends to make you warmer.

You can see that if fanning makes more muscle heat than you lose by faster evaporation of sweat, then fanning will actually make you warmer.

What would happen to a glass of water if you dumped it in space?

Christa Giordano
Philadelphia, Pennsylvania

I think it would just seem to explode and disappear. Space has a condition that you can call a "high vacuum"—almost no air at all. All those water molecules suddenly would have no more neighbors to bump into, so they would just fly apart in space.

How are shooting stars made?

Bobbie Petersen
Tracy, California

Most of the stuff in our solar system is in big bodies: the sun and planets and moons. There are also some rather small pieces of stuff as small as grains of sand or as large as big boulders. They are called meteoroids. I guess you can think of them as the trash of our solar system.

We know about meteoroids because some of them are on paths that make them run into our earth. Then the friction of the earth's atmosphere makes them white hot. We see them for a second or so until they vaporize, or burn up. That is the pretty sight you call a meteor or a shooting star.

Once in a while a big meteoroid does not all burn up and a piece of it falls all the way to the ground. The piece that is left is called a meteorite.

Why are there constellations?

Michelle Trautman
Scotts Valley, California

I'm not sure just how to answer your question. You did not ask why there are stars. Really, you want to know why people invented certain patterns out of the stars that we know as constellations.

It's my guess that people have always been fascinated by the heavens. Back when life was simpler, people generally lived by the sun, working during daylight hours. Many people were in close touch with nature. Surely a great many spent evenings talking with their friends and amusing themselves. One of the ways they passed their time at night, no doubt, was looking at the stars. I'll bet they found it fun to make up constellations.

I like to imagine a shepherd out guarding his flock on a lonely hill passing the time by thinking about certain patterns he saw. These patterns came to be shared by a number of people through the years and are now fairly common. But if you think about it, you could really make up your own.

How does a magnet attract metal?

Andrea Caron
Greenfield Park, Quebec

Actually, magnetism is a special property found in only a few metals, especially in iron and somewhat in cobalt and nickel.

Magnetism is a big subject, but maybe I can give you some ideas about it.

There is an important relationship between electricity and magnetism. Electricity is the movement of electrons. Any moving electron behaves as if it has a magnetic field—a cloud of magnetism—around it.

In all atoms there is a central nucleus with outer electrons spinning around in an orderly way. Different kinds of elements have atoms with different numbers and arrangements of those outer electrons. Do those spinning electrons create magnetic fields? We believe that they do. However, in most kinds of atoms the spins of the many electrons do not work together. You could say that they cancel each other so that the whole atom is not magnetic.

In an atom of iron it just happens that some of its electrons spin together just right. Their effects add together and the whole atom or a cluster of atoms behaves as a small magnet. A whole iron or steel bar behaves as a magnet if we can get all its little clusters of atoms lined up just right and working together.

You can think of any magnet as having a magnetic field or "cloud of magnetism" around it. If a piece of iron is close by, it is drawn toward the magnet. Maybe we can think that the atoms of that piece of iron are lined up, sort of soak up the cloud, and are pulled toward the magnet.

The ideas of magnetism make up a big and fascinating subject which I hope you will study. Someday, when you have learned a great deal more about it, you will think that the explanation I gave you here is way too simple.

Can you make gold from natural resources?

Heather Browning
Orland Park, Illinois

Very simply, the answer is no. Gold is one of the elements, and one of the important ideas of chemistry is that you can't change one element into another. There are some exceptions to this in the radioactive elements and in the special conditions that happen in the very high temperatures of stars. But gold is not one of the exceptions.

The modern idea about the elements was learned two hundred years ago. The science of chemistry grew out of an older practice called alchemy which had gone on for more than a thousand years. One of the main goals of alchemy was to make gold from other materials.

No one has been able to make gold out of anything else, even though people tried for over a thousand years. So I don't think you want to try it.

Why does metal feel cooler than wood when both are the same temperature?

John Fuery
Oakland, California

Some materials, like most metals, are good conductors and allow heat to flow very easily. Other things like wood and glass and Styrofoam are poor conductors.

When you touch something cold it feels cold because it takes some heat away from your hand. So you can see that a good conductor like aluminum takes heat away faster than a poor conductor like wood.

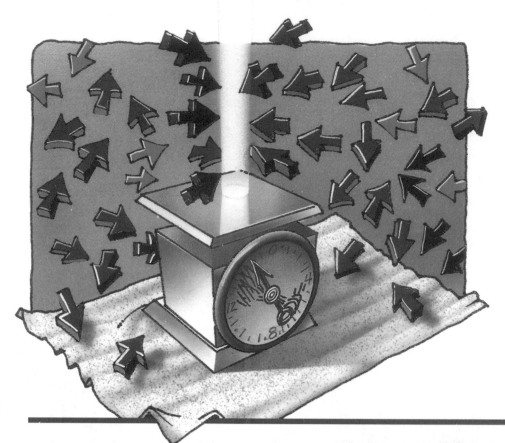

Since air is matter, does gravity hold the air down around us?

Jessica Bassett
Wellfleet, Massachusetts

The answer is yes. Our blanket of air actually is a weight pressing against the earth. We say that the air around us has a pressure of fifteen pounds per square inch. (A square inch is an area just about the size of a fifty-cent piece.) We could also say that all the air above each square inch of the earth's surface weighs fifteen pounds. That is a measure of the effect of gravity on air.

I would like to know how the earth floats in space and doesn't fall like a ball would fall.

Alicia Saylor
Hollsopple, Pennsylvania

If the earth were really alone it would actually just float in space. There would be no place to fall to.

But the earth is not alone. Fortunately it is locked into an orbit around the sun, held there by the force of gravity. You can think of the earth's motion this way. It is always trying to fall toward the sun. But because it is whirling around the sun in a circular path, it is also always trying to whirl out into space. Those two forces work against each other perfectly to keep the earth in its orbit.

When you are sitting on a bike with your feet off the ground and not pedaling, why does the bike tend to fall?

April Billet
Quartz Hill, California

Of course you always have to balance yourself when you are on a bike. That's easy when you are pedaling, but harder when you are stopped. When you are pedaling, the wheels are spinning. That makes your bike a gyroscope. A wheel spinning in an upright position tends to keep that position.

That same idea also works for other things. You have noticed that a spinning top falls over when it stops spinning.

So here's a question for a trivia game: how are bicycles and tops alike?

If we had no gravity, would a balloon fall to the ground?

Haley Shupe
Amanda, Ohio

You know that a balloon floats upward if it weighs less than the same volume of air. Weighing less means that the pull of the earth's gravity is less. If there were no such thing as gravity, there would be no force of gravity pulling on the balloon. So the balloon would not fall to the ground. That's one way to answer your question.

In our everyday lives we see the effect of gravity as a force pulling everything toward the center of the earth. However, you should remember that gravity is an important property of matter that works everywhere. Every body attracts every other body.

So we ought to consider that there is a lot more to your "what-if" question. If there were no force of gravity our world would be very different. There would be nothing to hold a blanket of air around the earth. In fact, there could be no earth if there were no force of gravity to hold it together.

The force of gravity is such an important part of nature that it is hard to imagine how things would be without it.

Why can't we see the minerals in the ocean until the water evaporates?

Kathy Steele
Guymon, Oklahoma

Seawater is a solution. That means that all the molecules present move around so happily together that there are no boundaries between different parts. That's another easy way of saying that inside the solution there are no places that can bend or reflect light. So the solution is perfectly clear.

If we take the water away by letting its molecules escape into the air, then the salts are left behind as crystals. Now there are boundaries at the surface of each crystal and it's easy to see the salts.

When a quart of seawater loses all its water by evaporation, it will leave about an ounce or about a tablespoon of salt. Most of that is sodium chloride, the same stuff that is in the saltshaker on your table.

How come when you put water on sand it moves a little bit, but then freezes?

Kathy Latirira
Barre, Vermont

That's an interesting observation. You noticed a special property of sand-water mixtures. It even has a fancy name: thixotropy. In a stirred or flowing sand-water mixture the sand particles act like independent little balls. Once the movement stops, the sand particles settle together in a "comfortable" position and stick to each other. They become so firm that they are sometimes called a gel, meaning something almost solid like gelatin.

Some kinds of sand do this more readily than others. Now you know what makes "quicksand" behave as it does.

I was at the Smithsonian space exhibit, and I am wondering how they freeze-dry space food.

Lee Anne Meck
Lititz, Pennsylvania

Freeze-drying is a special way of drying stuff. First you freeze it very rapidly at low temperature. The idea is to turn all the water quickly into very tiny ice crystals. Then you pump all the air away and keep the food in a vacuum. Then water molecules leave the ice crystals as water vapor without ever forming liquid water.

Ordinary drying with heat changes most foods so that they never feel or taste the same again. Freeze-drying gives a very dry stuff which becomes just like the original food when the water is put back.

You might like to know that very tiny organisms like bacteria can be preserved for years by freeze-drying. Then they can be made to grow again just by adding water. However, this works only for tiny one-celled organisms. Part of the trick is freezing very quickly to keep ice crystals very small so they don't damage membranes and structures inside the cells.

How come fresh water doesn't mix with salt water?

Caleb VanderHorst
Maumee, Ohio

Actually, fresh water and salt water do mix—but not very rapidly, especially if the fresh water is on top. Because salt water has all that dissolved salt, it is more dense (heavier). That makes it go to the bottom.

But if we wait long enough, the salt and water molecules keep moving around and mixing. That's called diffusion. In time the fresh water becomes saltier, and the salt water becomes fresher, until they are just alike.

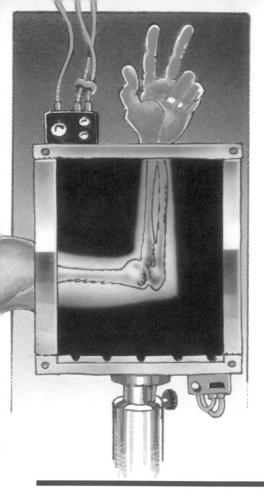

How come when you take an x-ray the skin doesn't show up?

Simone Seikaly
Salt Lake City, Utah

The answer depends on the nature of x-rays. They can be thought of as a very special kind of light, though a kind of light our eyes cannot see.

Light behaves as if it travels in little packets of energy called photons. Each photon of an x-ray has thousands of times more energy than a photon of ordinary light we can see. Because it has so much energy, it is hard to stop. Another way to say this is that x-rays are very penetrating.

Soft or less dense materials like paper or wood or rubber do not stop many x-ray photons. Most of them go on through. Hard and more dense materials like rocks or metals or bones are more likely to stop x-rays. So an x-ray photograph just shows the shadows of the more dense materials that were in the way. Skin and blood and muscle are not nearly as dense as bone. So an x-ray photograph usually shows most clearly the shadows of the bones.

If we can correct people's eyesight with glasses, can't we make glasses that have x-ray vision?

Naomi Cohl
Oakland, New Jersey

It is fun to think about being able to wear glasses that would allow you to look right through things by seeing x-rays. There is a very simple reason why this would never work in everyday life.

Our eyes see light only when there is light around us. The eyes do not put out anything. They are only receivers and detectors of light. During the day there is lots of light around us, but at night we have to use lamps to make light if we want to see.

The amount of x-radiation around us is very small—too small even to measure. Of course we can make "lamps" to produce x-rays that are used medically to photograph bones in our bodies. But a whole lot of x-radiation is bad for us. If there were enough x-radiation around us to use for seeing, I doubt that there would be any humans or other living things on earth.

So I am happy just to be able to see with light.

232

Sometimes in the afternoon I see the moon. Why is this?

Alicia Mosialis
Woodbury, Minnesota

The moon is going around the earth in a big circle all the time. We can see it only when it is up above our side of the earth. And we see it because of the light that falls on it from the sun.

When the moon is up above us at night it seems to glow brightly because of the dark sky behind it. When it is up above us during the day it glows just as brightly. But then the sky behind it is so bright that we usually do not even notice it. You must have been looking carefully to see it in the afternoon.

What causes tides?

Kenneth Weaver
Grand Prairie, Texas

I can't tell you all about tides, but I can tell you the basic idea. The tides are caused by the effect of the force of gravity of the moon. The actual pull of the moon's gravity isn't very great. You can't feel the moon when it goes overhead, but it does have a small effect in a special way.

Since the earth is a solid body, the pull of the moon's gravity acts upon the center of the earth. The ocean is at the earth's surface, so it is four thousand miles closer to the moon than the core of the earth. So when the moon is overhead, it pulls on the water more than on the earth. This makes the water bunch up a little under the moon. That's what is called a high tide.

If you look up "tides" in an encyclopedia, you can learn a lot more about them.

233

I read an article about the South Pole. It looks freezing cold! If it is warm down south, why does it look so cold at the South Pole?

Karl Saxon
Mobile, Alabama

We are so used to living in the Northern Hemisphere that we forget to think about how things work in the Southern Hemisphere. You are correct that as you go south from where we live, the weather is likely to get warmer. That happens until you get to the equator. Then as you keep going south the weather is likely to get colder again as you get closer to the South Pole.

The coldest places on the earth are likely to be near the North and South Poles. Actually, I think the coldest place on earth is often somewhere on the continent of Antarctica, not very far from the South Pole.

If the world is round, wouldn't the people in the southern part be upside-down?

Katie Jagielski
West Allis, Wisconsin

The hardest part of getting used to the idea that the earth is round is that upside-down part. First you have to ask the meaning of "up" and "down."

The earth is a very large ball. Everything on it is pulled toward its center by the force of gravity. "Down" is "toward the ground," which is also toward the center of the earth. "Up" is away from the ground.

This works wherever you are, at every place on the earth's surface. There is no place you can stand on your feet on the earth's surface and be upside-down.

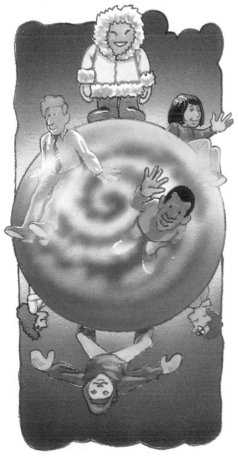

How do you get to China by digging a hole?

Lee Delattre
Ayer, Massachusetts

When you get to thinking about the earth as a big ball, you naturally begin to wonder about digging a hole through it from one side to the other. The idea of doing that is perfectly OK. The practical problem of doing it is so great that no one has ever tried in any really serious way.

One very practical problem is that the center of the earth seems to be a very hot molten mass that would melt any tools you can imagine using. And I guess it would cook anyone who was trying to use them.

So the idea of digging a hole through the earth probably will always be just an idea.

235

When we look at the sun, it's a big ball. Why do they say it's no bigger or different from any other star?

Margaret Malave
Carteret, New Jersey

Even though the sun is 93 million miles away, it still looks like a big ball. But it is not really unusually bright compared to other stars. It is just closer to us.

Other stars that you can see are likely to be brighter than the sun, but more than 100,000 times as far away. It is the distance that fools you. The universe is a big place.

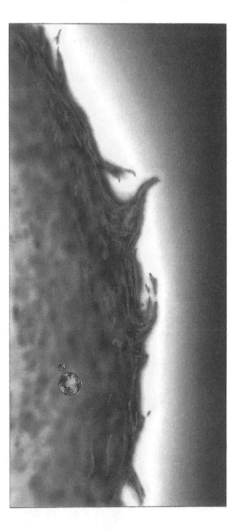

I would like to know if space ever stops.

Dorian Watson
Plano, Texas

That is about the biggest question in science, because the universe is the biggest thing we know of. I doubt that anyone really knows the answer.

I have read some ideas about this. One is that the universe is constantly expanding. Another is that space is really curved. I think this means that lines which seem straight to us must actually bend in the great distance of space and curve back to make great curves or circles. Another idea is that there is a real edge to the universe, but so far away no one could ever find it.

However, all of these are just ideas and I think the best answer to your question is that no one knows.

236

Why is it that when water comes down a waterfall it turns white?

Nancy Meadows
Crownsville, Maryland

I had never thought about that before so I wondered about it for a while. I am not sure of the answer, but I think it is something like this.

Light is reflected from a quiet pool of water as if the surface were a mirror. But if water is broken up enough into droplets, then there are many small pieces of water surface reflecting light at many different angles. Such a surface looks white.

You might think of glass that is clear and colorless. Some of the light that falls upon it is reflected from its smooth surface. But if the glass is ground or "frosted" to give it a rough surface, then it also looks white.

So I think that clouds and waterfalls look white because their water droplets make many little mirrors reflecting light in all directions. The many little water surfaces make what is called a diffuse reflector.

I've always wondered how the shape of a rainbow is formed.

Tom Harkman
Monticello, Minnesota

You also could ask why rainbows are always in the form of a bow or arc. Actually, they are always pieces of a circle.

A rainbow is made by rays of light from the sun which are bent and reflected by raindrops so that they come back to your eyes. Blue-violet light is bent more than red, so you see a band of light with all the colors in between spread out in order.

When you see a rainbow, the sun is always behind you and low in the sky. Imagine that you are holding your left hand in front of you so that it is in the shadow of your head. Now imagine that you use your right hand to point at the outer edge of the rainbow. And now keep your right hand pointing at the red part but move it back and forth from one end of the rainbow to the other. You will see that your right hand is moving in a circle. The angle between your hands will always be 42 degrees.

Why 42 degrees? That is the special angle at which red light comes back to you from raindrops. The only raindrops that can do that for you are at special places in the sky that make a circle. That's the circle which your right hand pointed to. Blue-violet light is bent at a smaller angle of about 40 degrees so it appears as a smaller, inside circle. Try that on your next rainbow.

If ultraviolet and infrared rays are invisible, how do we know about them?

Diana Foss
Huntington Beach, California

The best answer is that we know about them because of what they do. We have ways to detect and measure them.

Light that we can see is a very small part of what is called electromagnetic radiation. Radiation can be thought of as wave motion. We talk about different kinds of radiation which are really different only in how closely packed together their waves are. So we talk about their wavelength.

X-rays are very closely packed waves with short wavelength. And radio waves have a very long wavelength. In between there is the special region of wavelength where the radiation behaves like light. An even smaller region is one our eyes can see. That is what we call visible light.

Light that your eye can see comes in different colors, from the shorter wavelength violet, through blue, green, and yellow, to the longer wavelength red. So we say that light of wavelengths too short to see is ultraviolet (shorter than violet). And light of wavelengths too long to see is infrared (longer than red).

A radio can detect radio waves, and we have many gadgets that can detect and measure light. Seeing light with the eye is only one way we have of measuring it.

Why are the sky and water blue?

Lisa Marse
Metairie, Louisiana

The answers are not quite the same. The sky is blue because of the small scattering of sunlight by molecules of gases in the air, mostly by nitrogen molecules. We think of air as being very clear and transparent—and it is. We think of sunlight as being almost white—and it is. But in going thousands of miles through our atmosphere a tiny amount of sunlight is scattered. When that happens blue light rays are scattered more than red light rays—in fact about six times more.

So the light that is scattered down to us from the sky looks blue. I'm glad that happens. If it did not, the sky would look black.

Water is blue for a different reason. Of course when you look at the ocean or a big lake it may look blue partly because of light reflected back from the sky. But water is blue mostly because it *is* blue. You can't see this just looking through a glass of water. But try looking through the water in a clear lake or in a swimming pool that has white sides and bottom. If you look through enough clear water you will see that it is blue.

Water, even very pure water, absorbs red light rays a little more than blue rays. So water is a little bit blue.

239

When I sit by my window, I wonder how many different gases there are. Do you know all of the gases? I want to know.

Becky Lessing
San Antonio, Texas

If you look out the window at all the air around you, there is nothing to see. So what are all the gases out there?

There are a lot of gases in the air around us. Of course, most of the air is made up of just three gases—nitrogen, oxygen, and argon. There are smaller amounts of carbon dioxide and water vapor. And there are about ten more gases in amounts so tiny that people seldom talk about them. Of course, the list doesn't stop, either. Anything that you can smell—like roses or cheese or onions—must have some chemical that is carried as a gas in the air. So if you want to think of things like that, then the list of gases in the air would go on and on. I hope you do not want me to name them all because I doubt that anyone really knows.

Why doesn't the earth's oxygen get used up, since everybody breathes it?

Vivek Dehejia
Nepean, Ontario

You are right that we use up a lot of oxygen. Each person needs about five hundred quarts or over a pound of oxygen every day. If you think of all the people in the world doing that—and all the other animals, too—that's a lot of oxygen.

Fortunately there is a very neat answer to this problem. All of the green plants in the world are making oxygen. Not only that, but we animals are making the carbon dioxide that plants need. So plants and animals live happily together by swapping those two gases back and forth.

The concentration of oxygen in air is about 20.94 percent. That value has not changed in all the years it has been measured, so our recycling of oxygen must be working very well.

I was looking at our wood stove and I noticed that the flame was kind of blue. How come?

Rebekah Rooh
Forest Grove, Oregon

Most gases burn with a blue flame. Wood burns best when it gets hot enough to turn the wood into a gas, which then burns in the flame. Your wood stove must do a good job of burning wood.

I think you asked your question because we are used to seeing the yellow flames of an open bonfire. I think the yellow comes from glowing particles of carbon that are carried into the flame.

Why do things rust?

Melissa Riley
Oakville, Missouri

You may have noticed that rusty things are made of iron. When iron is in contact with air, it actually burns very slowly to make iron oxide. That's the red stuff you call rust. Things rust much more rapidly in the presence of water.

The reaction with oxygen can occur only at the surface of the iron. Then the rust usually crumbles away, and that makes more new surface. Given enough time, an iron object like a nail may turn completely to rust.

Other metals like aluminum also react with oxygen at the metal surface. But aluminum oxide sticks onto the metal and forms a protective coat.

241

Please explain why balloons float to the ground softly, like parachutes.

Ian Nichols
Canoga Park, California

When you blow up a balloon by mouth, it is full of air. The rubber doesn't weigh very much. The whole balloon is only a little heavier than the same volume of air. So it does sink to the ground. But as it sinks it must push a lot of air out of the way.

You might try this experiment. You need two rubber balloons that are just alike. Blow up one of them. Leave the other without being blown up. Now drop both balloons and watch how they fall. A balloon that's not blown up falls like most other objects, but the blown-up balloon just floats to the ground.

You are right about parachutes. Even when attached to a weight, they float down like a balloon because they must push away so much air.

Why do airplanes sometimes leave white streaks in the air?

Michelle Patano
Schaumburg, Illinois

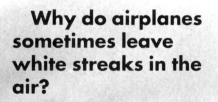

The engines of a jet plane are burning a lot of fuel. The burning process makes carbon dioxide and water. Most jets fly pretty high, like 35,000 feet, where the air is cold. The water vapor coming out of the jet engines rapidly condenses to form water droplets. So the plane forms a long narrow cloud behind it, which makes a white streak across the sky.

Sometimes, when there is enough water vapor in the high-up sky, another effect also takes place. The high-speed movement of the plane cools the air behind it enough to make the water vapor condense into tiny water droplets.

242

Why is a cast-iron pan heavy when I carry it by the handle and light when I carry it by the handle and the front part?

Sara Busby
Willow, Alaska

I think you have made an important observation. There are easier ways and harder ways to carry something. It is hard to hold a heavy pan by its handle if it is straight out in front of you. The muscles of your hand and arm must hold up the weight of the pan. They also must work extra hard to hold it in that awkward position. If you just hold the pan by its handle and let the pan swing downward, it will be easier to hold in that position.

The actual weight of the pan doesn't change. But your muscles have to work harder to hold it in some positions. If you watch workers who carry ladders or heavy bags of cement or heavy tools, you will see that they have special ways of carrying those things. They have learned to use the easiest way.

Is there any object in the world with only one side?

Gevonne Forguson
Sanford, Florida

I don't really know how to answer that because I am not sure just what you mean by a side. How many sides does a ball have? If we should decide that it has only one, then we would say that the whole earth has only one side. That is, unless you think about the idea of inside and outside.

I also thought about the Mobius strip that you may know about. It is easy to make.

Take a strip of paper, twist it once, and then tape its ends together. If you trace your finger along one side, you will touch every surface before coming back to the place you started from. So it has only one side. Of course, this is not quite fair because it also has one edge, which might be called a side.

I'm not sure whether I answered your question, but maybe you can have some fun thinking about it.

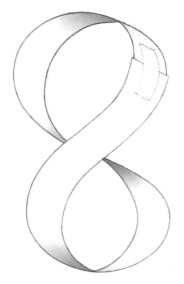

How is a car run by a motor?

Sarah Morgan
Myakka City, Florida

That's a big question. I can't tell you all about it, but I hope I can give you an idea.

You know that your car needs gasoline to run. The gasoline is turned into a gas or vapor, mixed with air, and carried into little chambers inside the motor. Then a spark is used to light the gas and explode it right inside each little chamber. Each explosion pushes on a crank and makes it go round and round. The sparks to the different chambers are timed just right so that they explode and push at just the right times. Then they suck in some more of the air and gas and get ready to do it all over again. That way they all work in perfect teamwork to make your car go.

Does sound travel in space?

Rachelle Theisen
Fargo, North Dakota

Sound is carried as a wave of compression in some material. The sounds we usually hear are carried by air. Space is close to a perfect vacuum, meaning there's almost nothing there. So sound does not travel in space. There is no sense in yelling at a star.

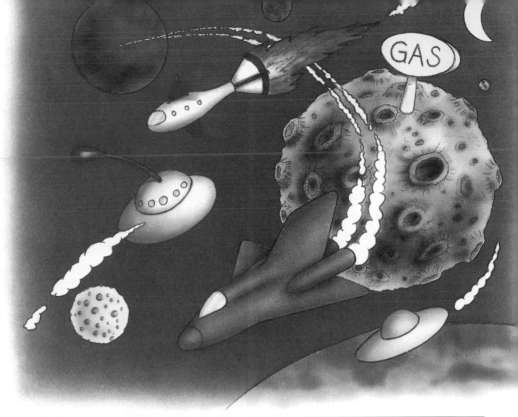

Why do we hear the sound of the ocean in seashells when they are dry?

Steve Swerdlow
Los Angeles, California

Seashells do not really make any sounds of their own. Inside they have many hard, curved surfaces which are good reflectors for sound. So any sound waves that get inside are jumbled up by all kinds of echoes. When you hold the shell up to your ear, you hear the noise of all those jumbled-up echoes. That does sound much like the noise of ocean waves beating against a shore.

If you have a seashell with a big cavity inside, try it out again at home next to your ear. Unless you get in a very, very quiet place, it will keep roaring as if it had brought some of the ocean with it.

How does smoke disappear?

Todd Fur-Marski
Manhattan Beach, California

Smoke is made up of tiny particles, usually of two kinds. One kind is made of ash, stuff not burned in the fire. The other kind of particles are tiny droplets of water which are formed when most things burn. Both kinds of particles must be small enough and light enough to get carried upward in the draft of hot air rising from the fire.

Each of the particles is too small for the eye to see. You see them as smoke only when there are lots of them together.

As the smoke rises above a chimney, it begins to mix with the air around it. The water droplets really do disappear because they evaporate to become water vapor.

The ash particles actually do not disappear. They just get farther and farther apart as they mix into the air. When they spread apart far enough they become part of the dust that is in the air all around us. They seem to have disappeared.

How does a camera put pictures on a piece of paper?

Robert Lopez
Leesburg, Indiana

You have noticed the lens on the front of a camera. It works to make an image on the back of the camera, a picture of what the camera is looking at. At the back of the camera is a film, a clear plastic sheet treated with special light-sensitive chemicals. "Light-sensitive" means that the chemicals undergo chemical reactions only when light hits them. Light-sensitive chemicals will make lighter and darker places on the film to form a picture.

These are only the basic ideas of how a camera works. You will find more about it in an encyclopedia, usually under "photography."

Why is it when you hold writing up to a mirror it is written backwards?

Nicole and Brad Van Pelt
Lisle, Illinois

The reason is that a flat mirror bounces light rays from an object back to you in straight lines. When you look in a mirror, the "you" you see is backwards, really reversed right and left.

Here's a way to check this out. Stand in front of a mirror and hold a penny out where you can see it in your right hand. Now look at yourself in the mirror. If you think about the person looking back at you, you will see that the hand holding the penny seems to be the left hand. In order to see why this happens, you must trace the course of a light ray from the penny to your eyes. The ray must go from the real penny to the point on the mirror where you see the penny and then back to your eye.

What we are talking about is called a mirror image. Because that image is reversed from the real you, a mirror cannot show you exactly how you look to other people.

247

Why do some cereals pop when you put milk on them?

*Eddie Fuhrman
Gillett, Arkansas*

Since I was not sure of an answer, I wrote to a company which makes breakfast cereals. Here is what they said:

Most cereal grains contain starch. It is possible to process the grains to make air pockets surrounded by starch. When starch gets wet it swells up. Then the air pockets break to give the popping noise.

I realize that this does not really tell us all that we would like to know. But at least we can understand the idea.

Our class has been studying science. I don't understand what inertia is and what momentum is.

*Lisa Matthew
Alamogordo, New Mexico*

The idea about inertia applies to movable things like balls and bats and cars and planes. Anything that is at rest stays at rest unless something else gives it a push. Then it is a moving body. And when in motion, it tends to keep moving in a straight line unless some force pushes or pulls to stop it or make it turn.

So the idea about inertia is simply that something tends to keep on doing whatever it is doing.

When something is moving it has momentum. The heavier it is and the faster it is moving, the harder it is to stop. So momentum is a kind of measure of how hard it is to stop something in motion.

In everyday life there is always some resistance to movement, which we call friction. Friction is like a drag or a pull against the direction of motion. This always works to slow down something in motion and make it come to rest again.

It always sounds complicated when we try to talk about things in very general terms. The best way to understand these ideas is to watch how movable things behave.

Sometimes when I am in the car it looks like there is water up ahead on the road. When I get closer, there isn't any water at all. Why?

Jill Biegler
Boca Raton, Florida

I have noticed that, too. I think you will find that it usually happens on a warm day when the sun is making the road surface hot. Then air is rising from the hot surface and other air is moving in to take its place. So there are a lot of hot and cool air drafts churning around close to the road surface. Light going through that churning air is bent back and forth to make the road surface look wavy—like a water surface.

On a hot day in the desert you might see even stranger things. They are called mirages—all kinds of strange things that seem to appear and disappear. Mixtures of churning air can bend light rays to give all sorts of strange effects.

249

My class did a science experiment with ice cubes. My group was freezing hot water and cold water to see which would freeze first. The hot-water cup froze first. The theory my group had for this was that the hot water underwent an extreme temperature change, therefore, the hot water froze first. Are we right?

Lee Ann Davis
Boulder, Colorado

In general, hot water will not freeze faster than cold water. In order to freeze hot water you have to take more heat away and usually that takes longer. So if hot water freezes faster, that is a surprise.

There are some special conditions under which hot water might freeze faster. Suppose you put exactly a pint of water in each of two identical pans and put the pans outside on a very cold day in the winter. Everything is alike except that one pan has hot water and the other pan has cold water. It is said that the pan of hot water will freeze first.

There are two possible reasons for this surprising result. First, water expands when heated. A pint of hot water really does not contain as many water molecules as a pint of cold water. So the pan of hot water will not make as much ice. Secondly, hot water will evaporate more as it is cooling down. Again this means that there will be less ice to freeze. So it is said that the pan of hot water will freeze first.

This experiment we talked about is supposed to have been reported first by a scientist, Roger Bacon, who lived in England about seven hundred years ago. I remember once reading a little article in a scientific magazine which said the experiment does not always work the way Roger said it did. The article was titled "Roger Bacon Was Mistaken."

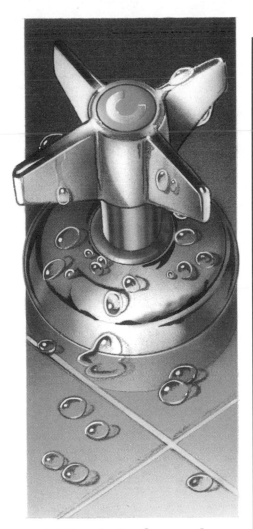

Why is it that when you leave a glass of cold pop out it gets warm, but if you leave a hot cup of cocoa out it gets cold?

Erin DeWald
South Bend, Indiana

The way you said that does make it seem like magic. Actually that's exactly what must happen. It all depends on the way heat behaves: it always flows from someplace hotter toward someplace colder.

For something hot like cocoa, the heat flows from the cocoa to the air of the room. So the cocoa cools down. If you leave it overnight it will become the same temperature as the surrounding air.

Room air is warmer than cold pop. So heat flows from room air to the pop, and the pop warms up. If you leave the pop overnight, it will have time to reach the same temperature as the surrounding air (and the cocoa).

You can see that heat behaves logically but not magically.

Why is it that when I take a shower, the cold water faucet has drops of water on it and the hot water faucet is all steamy?

Meg Hazel
West Columbia, South Carolina

When you are in a partly closed space (like a shower) with warm water, the air gets very humid. That means that the warm air has a lot of water vapor. If there is some cold spot, water condenses out of the air to form drops of water. You can see that this is likely to happen on the cold water faucet but not on the hot water faucet.

INDEX